The Parables of Paul

- THE MASTER OF THE METAPHOR -

J. ELLSWORTH KALAS

Abingdon Press / *Nashville*

THE PARABLES OF PAUL
THE MASTER OF THE METAPHOR

Library of Congress Cataloging-in-Publication Data

Kalas, J. Ellsworth, 1923-
  The parables of Paul : the master of the metaphor / J. Ellsworth Kalas.
First [edition].
    pages cm
  Includes bibliographical references.
    ISBN 978-1-6308-8253-2 (binding: soft back : alk. paper)   1. Bible. Epistles of Paul—Criticism, interpretation, etc.   2. Metaphor in the Bible.   3. Bible—Parables.   I. Title.
  BS2650.52.K35 2015
  227'.066—dc23

2014042724

15 16 17 18 19 20 21 22 23 24—10 9 8 7 6 5 4 3 2 1
MANUFACTURED IN THE UNITED STATES OF AMERICA

Dedicated to my special friends in the Sabbath School Back Side
Class at the Seventh Day Baptist Church in Alfred Station, New York

Contents

Contents

Introduction

S everal years ago I started a new year with a resolve to become better acquainted with the apostle Paul. I committed myself to a daily, unhurried early-morning meeting with Paul via the Book of Acts, to be followed later by his letters.

But before I even began reading, I made a list of things that I felt Paul had missed. After all, Paul didn't encounter Christ until his conversion on the road to Damascus, when he was confronted by the spirit of the risen Christ. He never saw Jesus in the flesh. Thus Paul described himself—perhaps somewhat ruefully—as one who was "born at the wrong time," which made him "the least important of the apostles" (1 Corinthians 15:8-9). It isn't surprising that many in the early church didn't consider Paul an apostle for the simple reason that he had never been part of the group that Jesus originally chose. This meant that he never saw Jesus heal the sick, raise the dead, or feed the multitudes. And of course he never heard Jesus excoriate the Pharisees; this might have been hard for Paul to have swallowed because one of the early goals of his life had been membership in that select, disciplined body. He never heard Jesus counter the religious leaders who tried to confuse him in public debate, always to their own embarrassment. I wonder how Paul, with his trained scholarly mind, would have responded to such occasions.

Nor did Paul ever hear Jesus teach or preach. Thus the man who became the church's first theologian actually quotes Jesus only once (Acts 20:35) and never alludes, for example, to Jesus' sublime proclamation that we call "the Sermon on the Mount." And of course Paul never heard some of the loveliest and most transforming stories ever told, the parables of Jesus. He never heard Jesus tell about the good Samaritan or the widow who pestered the unjust judge until he gave her justice or the lost sheep or the lost coin.

Then, suddenly but logically, something else struck me. Jesus, the Master Teacher, told stories, but Paul, Christianity's premier theologian, never told any stories; at least none are recorded for us. I smiled to myself at the thought of Paul saying, "A certain man had two sons" (Luke 15:11), or "A farmer went out to scatter seed" (Matthew 13:3). That just didn't sound like Paul!

But it was just then that I was confronted by Paul the story-teller, Paul the man of many parables. That is, Paul the Master of the Metaphor, the teacher who seemed almost always to have a metaphor that made his point graphic and accessible, made it easy for his listeners or readers to grasp basic concepts and to remember them. Matthew tells us that Jesus spoke to the crowds "only in parables" (Matthew 13:34). I submit that we might say of Paul, "he wrote his letters only in metaphors." I calculate that over these past nearly twenty centuries Paul's metaphors have provided a basis for millions of sermons by hundreds of thousands of preachers. Paul had the stuff of parables in his countless metaphors, but he never fleshed out a metaphor with a plot.

Perhaps just now you want to confess that you don't remember exactly what a metaphor is. You remember hearing the word some time ago (perhaps *quite* some time ago) in a high-school grammar class, but you've forgotten. Well, here's a good, brief definition from a responsible source: "A figure of speech in which a word or phrase is applied to a person, idea, or object to which it is not literally applicable. A metaphor is an implied analogy which imaginatively identifies one thing with another."[1] As it happens the author illustrates his point by a religious source, noting that Martin Luther used a metaphor when in his classic hymn he referred to God as "a mighty fortress" and a "bulwark." As for parables, our same source defines a parable as a "story designed to convey some religious principle, moral lesson, or general truth. A parable always teaches by comparison with actual events."[2]

So with something of an apology to a strict grammarian let me say that a metaphor is a picture looking for a story, or that a parable is a metaphor with a plot. Paul lets his metaphors stand alone. As a result he seems at times—sometimes more and sometimes less—to leave the interpretation of his metaphor to his reader. Paul's many metaphors are a kind of parable in shorthand. Jesus' parables generally have an easygoing quality about them, inviting us in for a chat. Paul's metaphors are more often like a car rushing by: jump on, if you can, while it passes—and if you hold on, it will give you quite a ride.

The metaphor is a strange literary critter. It makes things clear by giving us a picture. Thus when Luther says, "A mighty fortress is our God," I get a picture of God's protective power that is much more accessible than the theological term *omnipotence*. But metaphors also compel us to enter unexplored territory—and often without our realizing what they're doing. So when Paul says, "Put on God's armor" (Ephesians 6:11), he not only gives us a lively lesson for kindergartners but also opens the whole area of spiritual conflict, an area so profound that not many are comfortable exploring it.

Of course this is the essence of Paul, the theologian. He was a person raised in the tradition of the meticulous, imaginative Jewish rabbis but also trained in the Greek and Roman philosophers. He preached to congregations that he acknowledged had few wise or mighty among them, but he was unafraid when he met with the philosophical dilettantes on Mars Hill, a group that spent their time "doing nothing but talking about or listening to the newest thing" (Acts 17:21). Paul was a poet, as he shows so powerfully in 1 Corinthians 13, and he shows this repeatedly by his metaphors. They are not stories and they are not really parables, but they are pictures, and the longer we stand in Paul's gallery of metaphors the richer we become.

So I invite you to join me in what I hope you will find an exciting journey, as we walk with Paul through a few of his "parables."

The Slave: A Self-Portrait

Say what you will about Paul, he knew who he was. He was happy to recite his genealogical, academic, and religious résumé even as he disowned it. A number of his contemporaries (Paul never identifies them specifically) insisted that Paul wasn't an apostle because he hadn't been part of the original body of Jesus' disciples. Paul acknowledged that this was true and regretted that he was a latecomer, but he didn't let it get him down. Paul confessed that he didn't "deserve to be called an apostle" because he had persecuted the church (1 Corinthians 15:9); nevertheless he told those same people at Corinth that he wasn't "inferior to the super-apostles in any way" and that the people should know as much because through his ministry "the signs of an apostle were performed among you" (2 Corinthians 12:11-12). Paul knew who he was no matter what anyone might say otherwise. That's why it's interesting to see how Paul portrays himself when he tells us the kind of person he wants to be, and he does so with a picture. A metaphorical picture, that is.

We know Paul through two primary sources, the Book of Acts, where he is the lead personality in the latter half of the

book, and in his letters, which are such a significant part of
the New Testament. Most of those letters begin with what we
today would call a letterhead, the name and office of the writer;
and in our day, the address of the writer, including cell phone
and e-mail. If Paul were writing today, we'd see his name—
PAUL—in the center top line of a page, then perhaps centered
directly below or more likely a line or two down on the lefthand
side, we'd see his position. Where today someone might have
"President," "Director of Activities," or "Consultant," Paul most
often used the title that he loved above all others: APOSTLE. In
his letter to Philemon, Paul chooses the title "a prisoner for the
cause of Christ Jesus."

Apostle and *prisoner*: both terms were titles describing Paul's
role. The first title had come to him by divine authority and by
the recognition of many, though not all. The second came by
some of the circumstances of his work. It was something like
a twenty-first-century person who has fled from a tyranny and
identifies himself or herself as "a citizen in exile."

In several instances, however, Paul chose to adorn his letterhead with a metaphor, a word picture of himself by his own
choosing. He chose a powerful one. He used this metaphor in
his letterhead on three occasions, so we know it wasn't just a
passing mood or the reflection of some singular experience;
rather, it expressed something that was often on his mind. It
seems to me that it was the way Paul saw himself in his most
reflective moments.

He used it in his letter to the church at Rome, the epistle
that is usually seen as the most closely reasoned doctrinal exposition of all his letters. We could properly call Romans Paul's
scholarly paper. There he names himself "a slave of Christ Jesus,
called to be an apostle" (Romans 1:1). It's a strange and coun-

terintuitive combination. In it he ties the title he loves most and that he clings to in the face of all opposition, *apostle*, to a term that would seem not only to contradict that beloved identification but also to belittle it by association. "Slave" adds little but embarrassment to the title Paul cherished so highly. At the least it distracts, and at the worst it diminishes or contradicts.

Then there's Paul's letter to the people at Philippi. Philippi is generally seen as the church to which Paul felt the most intimate ties. He loved all of his people, no doubt about that; even in his occasions of strongest reproof Paul's love shines through again and again. But nothing to compare with the people at Philippi. This time Paul includes his young associate Timothy in the letterhead: "Paul and Timothy, slaves of Christ Jesus" (Philippians 1:1). I dare say that in including Timothy in this metaphor Paul didn't intend to belittle Timothy. He praises him unstintingly later in the letter, saying "I have no one like him" (Philippians 2:20). He sees Timothy as "like a son [who] works with his father" (2:22, adapted). I dare say that Paul is in the same mood and figure of speech when he includes Timothy with himself as "slaves of Christ Jesus." It's a good title for Paul, not a hurtful one.

Then there's the letter to Titus, another young associate. This letter is seen by scholars as either one of the last that Paul wrote, or as a letter written by someone close enough to Paul to feel justified in writing in Paul's stead, expressing Paul's thoughts. Here again Paul links the metaphor, slave, with his key letterhead title, apostle: "a slave of God and an apostle" (Titus 1:1). It is significant that in what is seen as either the last of Paul's letters or one written by someone who is conveying the last of Paul's thinking, that *slave* is again the letterhead word. The word, that is, that he saw as the climaxing description of who he was.

I'm no psychologist, but in years of receiving all kinds of correspondence (before the Internet took over a substantial share of written communication), I have developed an interpretive law: "By their letterheads you shall know them." Sometimes it is the title or the size of type or the choice of typeface, sometimes the placement on the page, and sometimes the amount of information accompanying the title; in some cases enough for a brief biography. As I said earlier, Paul knew who he was and needed no one to tell him. Further, he had lived with a wide variety of people, from scholars to shopkeepers to craftsmen to religious leaders to government officials, large and small, and to slaves. And when he chose a name for his letterhead that went beyond his office, *apostle*, or his temporary state, *prisoner*, he chose *slave*. If Paul had been able to have his picture on his letterhead as is now sometimes the case with the Internet, he would have chosen to portray himself with the garb and demeanor of a slave. He wanted to be seen and remembered as a *slave*. A slave of Christ Jesus, or of God.

If, then, you want to construct a parable in which Paul plays the lead role, begin it this way: "And behold, there was a slave..."

Paul knew a great deal about slaves. So did almost everyone in the first-century Roman world. In fact they knew slavery so well that I doubt that many thought about it very much. Slaves were a key part not only of the economy and of the workforce but also of the whole pattern of daily life; they were part of the social and economic landscape. In any given day the average resident of Rome might easily see more slaves than free persons. By responsible estimates, as much as half the population of Rome may have been slaves in Paul's time. This was not racial or ethnic slavery but an accompanying factor of war. Slaves were something that made war singularly profitable for the conquering nation and its people. When the Romans, with their practiced military skill, conquered some new territory, they brought home slaves of every kind, from those with the most menial skills to what today would be seen as professional ability. What better, in a wealthy home, than to have a slave who was your resident physician or lawyer or accountant—and also able, when necessary, to serve table guests at a dinner party. What better than to have a respected scholar as a daily tutor for your child.

But whether the slave was a physician or a gnarled laborer, he or she was still a slave. The owner had the power of life and death, and if the owner was a petulant, insecure person he could exercise that power by anything from daily humiliation to beatings or execution. Aristotle defined a slave as a piece of living property. When Paul chose to call himself a *slave*, he knew what the word meant. It was not a romantic phrase or a piece of philosophical poetry. Paul knew better than that. He knew slaves; they were among his converts. He also knew what he was saying when he wrote, "There is neither Jew nor Greek; there is neither slave nor free; nor is there male and female, for you are all one in Christ Jesus" (Galatians 3:28). People in the twenty-first century who critique Paul for not campaigning against slavery have no idea how radical a standard the apostle was laying out for the church and its relationships. But Paul knew what he was saying, and so did the original recipients of his letters.

And I repeat, so did Paul when he called *himself* a slave, and when he gave that title to Timothy, his beloved young associate. He knew that a slave's daily tasks and eventually his or her life or death depended upon the will (and whim) of the master. Nevertheless, he chose to call himself a *slave*; specifically, a slave of Jesus Christ.

This would be a daring word no matter in what setting Paul might have written it, but it is especially significant when the apostle uses it in his Letter to the Philippians. It's in this letter that Paul recites the dramatic description of our Lord's entry into this world. He reminds us that although Christ Jesus

> ...was in the form of God,
>   he did not consider being equal
>   with God something to exploit.
> But he emptied himself
>   *by taking the form of a slave*
>   and by becoming like human beings.
>   (Philippians 2:6-7; italics mine)

With that phrase, "by taking the form of a slave," Paul lets us know why he cherishes this metaphor-portrait of himself. By calling himself a slave of Jesus Christ, Paul is also telling us that he intends to be like Jesus Christ.

In another of his letters Paul tells us God's purpose in all the ministries of the church—those of apostles, prophets, evangelists, pastors, and teachers: it is that we will all become "mature adults—to be fully grown, measured by the standard of the fullness of Christ" (Ephesians 4:13). What is the goal of the Christian life? It is to become truly *mature*; that is, to become like Jesus Christ. And what is the fullest expression of maturity, of Christlikeness? To do what Christ did, to take the form of a slave!

See, then, that for Paul the slave-designation was not a title of humiliation or of abasement, but—of all things!—a title of achievement. This is Paul's declaration of maturity. He has grown up to the fullness of Christ, following his Lord to the greatness of complete, *willing* subjection to the purposes of God. By being a slave Paul is uniquely near to the image of Christ.

Paul had a further understanding of the role of a slave that wouldn't naturally occur to us. It came to him by way of his upbringing in the Hebrew Scriptures. In a culture centuries before Paul's time, the law of Moses had dealt in a straightforward way with a social and economic problem in their society. In severe economic circumstances a person (more likely a man) could sell himself into slavery to a fellow Hebrew. This "Hebrew slave" would serve for six years and then in the seventh year he would "go free without any payment" (Exodus 21:11).

But there was more to the contract. If he had gained a wife and children during the years of slavery, and if his experience with his master had been a very good one, he could "clearly [state], 'I love my master, my wife, and my children, and I don't want to go free,' then his master will bring him before God. He will bring him to the door or the doorpost. There his master will pierce his ear with a pointed tool, and he will serve him as his slave for life" (Exodus 21:2-6). Did Paul see himself as such a love slave? Was he finding his service for Christ so rewarding that he knew he could only make it better by choosing to see it as full slavery, made more beautiful by the piercing of his ear, so to speak, at the door of his master's house?

There is still another picture of slavery that was surely part of Paul's thinking when he chose to call himself a slave of Jesus Christ. It is a very different one. Where the pictures in Philippians and in Exodus are significant by favorable comparison, there is one in the Epistle to the Romans that is powerful by its contrast. Also, as with Paul's letter to Philippi, this allusion comes in an epistle in which Paul has made *slave* part of his letterhead. Some

novelist has observed that readers often find points of significance in a novel that the writer never had in mind, and it's easy
for us to do this in our reading of the Scriptures, so I don't want
to belabor the point I'm about to mention. But perhaps Paul
made his allusions in Philippians and Romans, letters where he
identified himself as Christ's slave, because the theme was so
strong in his soul at the time, as shown by the other material in
each letter.

In the letter to the Romans, Paul looks at slavery as he himself
has known it at its worst. He uses the word as a metaphor, and
an altogether ugly one. He wants the strongest word possible to
describe his experience in his relationship to sin. Paul's world
was no different from ours in its casual attitude toward sin. The
culture of his time was as adept as ours in excusing itself. One
of the things we learn from the biblical story in the garden of
Eden is that we humans have always had a remarkable ability
for self-excusing. Adam blamed his sin on Eve, and Eve blamed
hers on the serpent. Succeeding generations have continued per-
fecting this skill; some have been more sophisticated than others, and the first century of the Common Era was one of the
most accomplished in this matter. The relative prosperity of the
Roman Empire, its entertainment, its literary breadth, its comfort with crudeness in the midst of learning—all of these made
it easy to rationalize sin or to live comfortably with it.

Paul knew better. Part of his attitude was shaped by his
studies as a Pharisee. The Pharisees may often have majored in
minors, but at their best they realized that sin is humanity's key
problem. Certainly Paul's vigorous-but-failed attempts as a very
earnest Pharisee made him realize the power of sin. So Paul put
it sharp and clear: he was a *slave* to sin, and so are we all unless

we choose instead to become *slaves to righteousness* (Romans 6 and 7).

Paul was a tough-minded thinker. He believed that we humans are going to live for one thing or another and that the choices we make eventually lead to slavery. Most people, unfortunately, don't think about the matter long enough or seriously enough to see how controlling our patterns of thought and conduct eventually become. Paul knew the power of these daily choices, and he chose to become the slave of Jesus Christ.

A practical, pragmatic question remains. How do we live out this life as Christ's slave? If we take seriously our slavery to Christ, it means ready servitude to others. That is, it means giving up our rights in matters large or small in order to help others. If we choose such a life pattern, we can become victims of persons who live off of willing and helpful people; that is, we can become what counselors sometimes call "enablers," people who make it easy for others to avoid self-responsibility.

There's no universal answer for this problem because it shows itself in daily issues rather than in broad, philosophical categories. But as a principle of life Paul saw himself as the slave of Christ, and he lived out that slavery in his service to other persons; how else, after all, do we serve Christ than through people and through God's creation? This meant that, on occasions, service to one person made it impossible to serve another; to serve Christ is through persons, but sometimes decisions have to be made between those persons. At a pragmatic level, this is a matter of daily judgments. But as a principle our slavery to Christ is a life-commitment.

I have begun our study at this point because if we want to understand Paul's parables we need to begin by understanding Paul's person: getting inside Paul's set of mind and spirit. We have to know the basis for Paul's reasoning. This begins with Paul's self-image: Paul sees himself as a slave of Jesus Christ's. And he sees this slavery as a beautiful thing, a life to be pursued.

We begin our study of Paul with his letterhead where he calls himself a slave. It would be a holy achievement if we could finish our study claiming Paul's letterhead as our own.

The Christian Life as a Sports Fan Sees It

When I was a very young preacher I read a book on preaching written by an outstanding pulpiteer of the first quarter of the twentieth century. The author raised a question: "What does a preacher do when the congregation's attention is wandering?" His answer: "Take them out to the country." It was sound counsel for its time. In those days a substantial percentage of America's population was involved in agriculture, and those who were not had family or friends who were. Talk about farm life, and the odds were high that you would get the attention of your audience.

There is no longer such a dominant common denominator in America. Sports, however, might be the closest possibility. Football's Super Bowl is in a class by itself in the size of its television audience and the price of its commercials. College basketball has coined a name for a season: "March Madness." Baseball's World Series doesn't have its singular appeal, but it still ignites the enthusiasm of multiplied millions. Twice every four years the Olympics, alternating between the summer and the winter games, solicit attention around the globe. And of course I've just skimmed the surface: what about golf, tennis, soccer, and the organized leagues for boys and girls that begin at grade school and sometimes before?

When Jesus preached and taught in Galilee he spoke of the lilies of the field, of a lost sheep, of a treasure hidden in a field, and when he called men to follow him, it was with the challenge that he would make them fishers of men. But when Paul took the gospel to the urban world of the Gentiles, he spoke of wrestling and boxing and racing. He spoke as the man he was, one who had grown up in the world of the Olympics and of the Greek gymnasia. Paul saw himself as called to be the apostle to the Gentiles. We know that many others in Paul's time went into "all the world," as Jesus commanded, but no one was as qualified to do so as Paul, who was born in the city of Tarsus, and who knew the Gentile urban world just as he knew the Greek and Roman philosophers and poets.

It was a world of sports. Not to the measure of our times, especially with what radio and television have done to multiply sports audiences, but it was pervasive enough and captivating enough to provide an apt speaker like Paul with figures of speech and metaphors that were part of the everyday conversation of his listeners and readers.

The Greeks led the way in public sports, the Olympics having started some several centuries before Christ. But the Olympics were a particular expression of a pervasive, daily love of sports and bodily grace. Other ethnic groups found this Greek enthusiasm strange at best. Anacharsis the Scythian reported after visiting Greece, "In each city there is a place set apart in which the Greeks act insanely day after day!"[1] Anacharsis's language reminds us that our term *fan* is an abbreviation of *fanatic*. Perhaps it isn't surprising that the appetite for excitement made the public games more and more violent, until in some of the human combats, and the battles between human beings and starved animals, the show didn't end until death for one or more of the participants. Paul didn't refer to that kind of sports, although violence in entertainment was becoming more popular during his lifetime. His references were confined to competition at a less brutal level.

The apostle uses the language of sports in an almost casual way, just as many of us do today; some of his are lost in translation. His longest single use of sports metaphors is in First Corinthians. No wonder! The Isthmian games were held close to Corinth, so the Corinthians laid claim to them, just as in our day people in an extended region claim particular athletic teams as their own. The Isthmian games dared to be held every two years, while the Olympics were quadrennial, which added to the Isthmian audience.

The Isthmian games included races, wrestling, jumping, boxing, and javelin and discus throwing. Paul mentions two of these in his letter to the Corinthians and refers to the whole event the way a present-day speaker would refer to the Super Bowl or the World Series.

> Don't you know that all the runners in the stadium run, but only one gets the prize? So run to win. Everyone who competes practices self-discipline in everything. The runners do this to get a crown of leaves that shrivel up and die, but we do it to receive a crown that never dies. So now this is how I run—not without a

clear goal in sight. I fight like a boxer in the ring, not like someone who is shadowboxing. Rather, I'm landing punches on my own body and subduing it like a slave. I do this to be sure that I myself won't be disqualified after preaching to others. (1 Corinthians 9:24-27).

Preachers sometimes err by using a metaphor or an illustration that diminishes the significance of the point they're trying to make. Paul makes sure this doesn't happen. His people at Corinth know that the races are a big deal, big enough that Paul will employ them to his purposes; nevertheless, however, the races and other events are far, far less than the race in which we Christians compete every day, through all of our lives. "So run to win," Paul cries. This race is not for the casual athlete or the dilettante; it is for those who intend to win the crown.

Now Paul uses his metaphor to the limit. In the Greek races the winner received a crown made of pine boughs and often of *selinon*, an herb similar to parsley or celery. By the time an athlete had returned home, his crown was wilting and turning brown. Not so, Paul said, with the crown for which we Christians strive; ours is a crown "that never dies."

I'm sure Paul had as hard a time convincing his people at Corinth as Christian teachers and preachers have in our day. If a neighbor came home with an Isthmian crown made of withered leaves, the Christian neighbor no doubt viewed it with awe and perhaps envy. Did they have the same sense when a fellow believer reported progress in her devotional life or victory over a besetting sin? Even though such victories are mostly issues of only a given day, their content is eternal.

When you watch spectacular ice-skating in the Winter Olympics or skiers who seem oblivious to danger as they sail through the air, you comment to a fellow viewer that such skill demands thousands of hours of intense preparation. If they win, there will be a moment of glory on the awards platform and very possibly some endorsement contracts and perhaps professional entertainment contracts. But even those who lose are likely to say that the opportunity was worth the huge investment of time, money, energy, and emotion. I honor them for the skills that make them breathtaking performers, and the self-discipline that drives them to such unceasing hours of practice, practice, practice—including also so many failures, failures, failures.

But I wish we believed Paul when he reminds us that such rewards are temporary. The Olympics give gold, silver, and bronze medals, headlines and adulation, and often, for a period of time, financial rewards. But with all of that, they still are not eternal. They are part of a world "where moth and rust eat them and where thieves break in and steal them" (Matthew 6:19). No matter, we find it hard to believe that godliness is worth the effort. Athletes practice all kinds of self-denial to win a place in the Olympics. Not many Christians practice a comparable level of self-denial to achieve godliness. I sense the apostle's sorrow as he compares the dedication of his Corinthian believers with that of the athletes just down the road in Isthmia.

But Paul is wise enough to know that the people to whom he preaches and writes are no more in danger of spiritual shallowness than he is himself. He now turns his Olympic metaphor from racing to boxing. The best thing I know about Paul's religion is that he rarely if ever thinks of himself more highly than he ought to think. Paul has watched the Olympiad boxers. He has seen them in the ring with an opponent, and also in preparation, when they shadowbox with imaginary opponents. It's easy to knock out an imaginary opponent and quite another matter when the opponent is set on one's own destruction.

Gregory of Nyssa was one of the great theologians of the fourth century. A twenty-first-century theologian, Michael Glerup, has translated some of Gregory's sermons into contemporary English. Gregory writes, "As a fighter, [Paul] was light on his feet and kept a close eye on his opponent's onslaught....He didn't merely shadow box, he attacked his opponent, pounding his opponent's body with hard-hitting blows....look at the shiner and the bruises he gave his opponent."[2]

But here is the remarkable thing about Paul. As he watches the boxers at work, he recognizes that his most dangerous opponent is himself. It is not the perpetrators of false doctrine, and not even hell itself, it is his own body, mind, and person. He is especially conscious of the struggles of the flesh, the temptations resident in his own body. So when we might expect Paul to pummel spiritual opponents both seen and unseen, he tells us that, "Rather, I'm landing punches on my own body and subduing it like a slave." Why? Because, he tells us, "I want to be sure that I myself won't be disqualified after preaching to others" (1 Corinthians 9:27).

A colleague who taught at the seminary where I serve used to tell new classes at the seminary (an institution that prepares its students to be ministers and professional church workers), "By coming here you have reduced by half your chances of getting to heaven." He intended to shock but also to make a hard point: the religious worker deals with spiritual hazards that are all the more dangerous because they are so artfully hidden. Thus, rightly, Paul feared that he would be "disqualified after preaching to others." He realized that his own body—and his mind and psyche as well—constituted the opponent facing him in eternity's boxing match. So he didn't shadowbox with imaginary opponents or smile indulgently on his occasional thoughts of lust or self-pity or pampered arrogance. Nor did he amuse himself by the kind of self-indulgence in which we make ourselves a character in an imaginary novel, fascinated by our own complexity. Paul landed fierce punches on his person, "subduing it like a slave." Paul had seen the clever, deceptive, effective moves of Olympic boxers, and he knew that we humans are engaged daily in just such a contest. Except for this crucial difference, that the contest we face has eternal consequences. There is no other quite like it. Unfortunately, it's easy to miss this eternal factor because the battle of the soul is fought out daily, and most of the time in ordinary circumstances, in what seem to be ordinary issues. It's hard to realize that all of the dusty minutiae of life is part of our eternal race, our ultimate battle. Unlike the Olympics or the Super Bowl, we don't often have an announcement that our game is played with such high stakes.

As Paul senses that he may be approaching the end of his earthly journey, he draws still more passionately on the images of sport, especially that of the race. His letter to the Philippians is one of his jail epistles. The Roman courts sought for justice, especially for those like Paul who held Roman citizenship. But Paul knows well enough that any day fickle human judgment could turn against him. As he contemplated that possibility, Paul appealed to his converts to hold steady because if they do so it "will allow me to say on the day of Christ that I haven't run for nothing" (Philippians 2:16). Paul had seen runners who lost the race; he didn't want to be one of them.

And Paul wanted his converts and those whom he had nourished in the faith to realize that they were an essential part of whatever victory he might finally achieve. If these believers failed to finish their respective races, it would mean that Paul's race itself had been "for nothing." Paul makes the point still more emphatic farther on in the letter, when he speaks of these people "whom I love and miss" as "my joy and *crown*" (Philippians 4:1, emphasis added). The inference is clear to his readers, people who had followed the Olympics and similar races and who knew how much the "crown" meant to the winner. Paul sees *them*, his polyglot of rich and poor, male and female, slaves and free, as his *crown*, as the ultimate evidence that he has won his race. For first-century sports enthusiasts, Paul couldn't have paid a more satisfying compliment.

In the Philippian letter, death is enough of an option that Paul contemplates the end of his race could be near. By the time we get to his Second Letter to Timothy, he feels that the end is very near. It is time now to look back on how he has invested his life in Christ and to contemplate its worth. As a pastor I've had hundreds of such conversations, both brief and extended, with persons contemplating retirement from their careers and others who were facing death; and now as a person of extended years I have my own reasons to evaluate the score in the game. I empathize with Paul as he writes.

So Paul tells Timothy, who still has most of his race before him, how he feels when "death is near": "I have fought the good fight, finished the race, and kept the faith. At last the champion's wreath that is awarded for righteousness is waiting for me" (2 Timothy 4:7-8). I'm not surprised that Paul makes such a faith statement by metaphors because figures of speech are so much his vehicle of expression. But I'm impressed that he relies so heavily on metaphors from the world of sports. He could have drawn from the world of scholarship or from his experiences in leatherwork and tent-making or from family life. Or he could have spoken in military pictures; anyone in the first-century Roman world would have understood such metaphors. Instead, he chose the world of sports—the boxer, the person in a race, the awarding of a winner's crown—to describe his feelings as he considered that his life was probably very nearly over.

And with one sweeping phrase, he noted a difference between the races of this world and the eternal race. Only one person wins the gold in boxing or running, but as Paul looks off toward his reward he speaks a grand promise to every believer. He is confident that on that unique day not only will he be welcomed as a champion, but it will also be so for "all those who have set their heart on waiting for his [our Lord's] appearance" (2 Timothy 4:8).

You may wonder how it is that Paul said nothing about team sports. Our contemporary culture has made "teamwork" a nearly sacred term in the world of business, government, education, and beyond. But in the first-century athletic world the competition was in individual sports; team sports were essentially unknown.

There is no one sport that appeals to everyone, and it's possible that there are some who dislike all sports—perhaps partly because they have reacted to sports fanatics. But Paul had found a venue that he knew would appeal to the Grecian culture where he had most of his ministry. Whether he was in Corinth, Philippi, Ephesus, or Rome, he knew he would be understood if he took his listeners to a stadium. And obviously, he himself was at home there.

He respected the dedication of athletes, and I think he understood the excitement of the fans who cheered them on. But he wondered how a person could watch an athletic event or participate in one and not realize that its reward—a crown that withered before the week was out or fame that lasted a few months or years—was hardly to be compared with God's reward. There was more to life than a runner's trophy.

I'd like it if Paul could be the guest commentator at the network covering the Winter or Summer Olympics. I can hear him say, "The gold medalist was at her best today. She demonstrated the results of years of training and self-discipline. Beautiful stride, excellent pacing, strength for the last dozen meters. I congratulate her.

"But there's more to us, you know, than muscle, and energy, and coordination. We are eternal creatures. Our biggest race is the one where God is the primary audience and the only Judge."

3

Sin and I

The world in which you and I live doesn't prepare us to discuss sin with the apostle Paul. Come to think of it, our world doesn't prepare us to discuss sin with Paul even when he was still Saul of Tarsus. Long before Christ had apprehended Saul on the road to Damascus, young Saul had a vigorous understanding of sin. He strove early to qualify as a Pharisee and, say what you will about pharisaical legalism and narrow-mindedness, they took sin seriously. So Saul of Tarsus was well-grounded in his understanding of sin years before he came to believe in Jesus Christ.

But in its own way, even the pagan world of Paul's time had an issue with sin. The daily Greek and Roman culture may have become comfortable with sin, but they had a philosophical heritage to challenge their conduct in at least a measure. Their philosophers believed there was a moral law, and they taught their followers the innate importance of such a concept. They had trouble defining and applying particular aspects of these moral laws, and trouble living them out, but the sense of right and wrong was strong among these so-called pagan philosophers.

This isn't necessarily so in our twenty-first-century world. J. Budziszewski, professor of government and philosophy at the University of Texas, notes that the neo-pagan (which is his name for many in the twenty-first-century Western world) "pretends, when it suits him, that there is no morality, or perhaps that each of us has a morality of his own." No wonder, then, that the pagan in Paul's world felt the need to be forgiven, while our neo-pagan contemporary "thinks the way to have peace is not to have the weight lifted but to learn not to take it seriously."[1]

Probably not many who are reading this book would classify themselves as neo-pagans. By your involvement in this study, you indicate that you feel there is a moral code and probably that you try to live by one. Still more, the code by which you seek to live is probably close to the biblical code. Nevertheless, it's difficult to live within a culture and not absorb something of its attitudes. This isn't necessarily an intentional acceptance; it's just that if we hear a tune sung often enough, we begin gradually to hum it ourselves without knowing that we're doing so. We take on the thinking of our culture in some measure and often more than we realize.

So we may not be ready for Paul's vigorous language when he discusses sin. We have found comfortable synonyms, so *sin* is hardly ever used in our daily secular conversation. What is worse, we may feel uneasy when we hear sin mentioned in church. Only the most heinous conduct seems to us to be really *wrong*. Some conduct may be personally offensive to us, and we wish people weren't like that, but we hesitate to call such a person a *sinner* or to refer to their conduct as sinful. And of course we don't easily use the term *sinner* to describe ourselves; if we do, it's probably with a knowing smile, to let others know that the word is more playful than descriptive. It's not surprising that the "confession of sin" that was once a part of the custom-ary ritual in most churches is no longer included in our usual pattern of worship except perhaps for its place in the service of Holy Communion.

But sin was a reality to Paul, and his parable of sin, his meta-phor, is a powerful one. It is, in fact, outright repulsive—and intentionally so. Paul knew the power of words; he was widely read in several languages, and he knew how to use the language of the scholars when he thought it was necessary. But he was also a man of the marketplace and of the sports arena and of the urban culture of his time, and the vigorous language of the common life often rose to the fore in his writing. So it is when he deals with a major fact of the human soul, sin. He knew sin as a life-and-death subject in his own life, and he found a metaphor to convey his parable.

It comes in his Letter to the Romans, as he lets us into his own spiritual journey and the struggles he has known and con-tinues to know. He puts it directly: "I don't know what I'm doing, because I don't do what I want to do. Instead, I do the thing that I hate" (Romans 7:15). This inner contradiction is so powerful that he realizes he is a divided personality. "The desire to do good is inside of me, but I can't do it. I don't do the good that I want to do, but I do the evil that I don't want to do. But if I do the very thing that I don't want to do, then I'm not the one doing it anymore. Instead, it is sin that lives in me that is doing it" (Romans 7:18-20).

As Paul struggles to find words to describe the state of his soul and conduct, he does what any able poet, essayist, novelist, or preacher is likely to do: he searches for a metaphor, a picture that will help the hearer or listener get the idea, to help him or her not only grasp it intellectually but also feel it emotionally—

and perhaps, thereby, be transformed spiritually. "I'm a miserable human being. Who will deliver me from this dead corpse?" (Romans 7:24).

Professor Craig Keener tells us that the phrase usually translated "Wretched person that I am" (here translated "miserable human being") was "a standard cry of despair, mourning or self-reproach," that it often appears in laments of that time, and that some philosophers of that period complained that they were imprisoned in a mortal body.[2] Paul has carried the idea a step further in his almost grisly metaphor: he says that he is forced to carry about a corpse. Our CEB translation, a "dead corpse," is of course redundant; what else is a corpse but dead? Apparently the translator is trying to convey to us the frustration Paul feels as he seeks language strong enough to describe his dreadful state; "corpse" is not emphatic enough to carry his experience; it is a "*dead* corpse."

Nor is Paul speaking simply of his own experience. He knows that he is discussing an experience that is common to great numbers of people, especially those who aim for a high moral standard, and particularly persons who are seeking a victorious Christian life and who feel defeated in their quest. Obviously Paul thinks that he's writing to persons who understand what he's talking about because they're living with the same appalling struggle. I sense that he writes in hopes of a double therapy: by his testimony he will lead his readers to peace even as he gains freedom for his own soul.

Understand that Paul is not thinking at this point of those persons who are trying to flee from God and can't do so. This is not the cry of the psalmist who wonders, "Where could I go to get away from your spirit? / Where could I go to escape your presence?" (Psalm 139:7), or the British poet Francis

Thompson, who tells us in "The Hound of Heaven" that he fled God "down the nights and down the days," and "down the labyrinthine ways" of his own mind, hid from God "in the mist of tears…and under running laughter." Not at all! Rather, Paul is describing the person who wants with full being to know God and to do God's will but who discovers that something else is at work in the soul; this something else is like carrying a "dead corpse."

So here is the unnerving part. Paul is describing the experience of someone who wants to please God. Paul wanted nothing so much as to please God in his own life and, by projection, in the lives of those whom he had brought to faith. Further, Paul was seeking something that God wanted him to have; what could God want for us more than purity of life and character and conduct? Yet something was in the way, this dreadful thing called sin. Looking for a picture that was adequate to the subject, he found nothing so apt as this, the burden of carrying a corpse day after day, week after week.

Such an idea was especially repugnant to the people to whom Paul was writing at that moment, the believers in Rome. Margaret R. Miles writes, "Corpses [in Roman society] were considered ill-omened"; thus the Romans were bewildered by the way Christians saw to proper burial of bodies not only of believers but of those neglected by society in general. The cultured Romans believed that "it is the mind that is to be honored and cultivated, while the human body must be ignored, disparaged, and 'scorned.'"[3] If Paul intended to shock his readers in Rome by his example, he surely was succeeding. True, these readers were Christians, but they were Christians who had imbibed fully in the culture patterns of Rome, and the idea of carrying a corpse was offensive in the extreme. And of course

Paul knew the Levitical laws about the ritual uncleanness that came from touching a dead body. So Paul knew that he was treading on sensitive ground with his figure of speech.

And this was exactly his point. He wanted a metaphor that would trouble—yes, shock—his hearers and readers because he wanted them to know how horrendous sin is. And if sin in general is horrendous, it is many times more so for the believer. Sin is a serious matter.

No wonder, then, that in a culture like ours we're comforted by the blurring of standards. We are encouraged always to see ourselves in the best light and to feel that at heart we're all OK. We mean well, and while it's unfortunate that we don't always do well, nevertheless, we should be judged by our best intentions rather than by our unfortunate lapses. If the list of "sins" is getting shorter as a result of our more enlightened, more broadminded attitudes, we think this is all to the good. Well, sometimes we think otherwise when the blurring affects issues that are important to us personally, but on the whole we find it easier to play life's game when the ball is not so often ruled out of bounds.

What kind of metaphor would we have for sin in our day? Paul saw sin as a corpse; what would our metaphor be? Perhaps, "Sin is like a golf ball that just misses the hole." The failure leaves us disappointed with ourselves, but fortunately another hole is coming up and we can do better next time. Or perhaps, "Sin is a poor choice." This is one of the most popular phrases in our culture, especially when an athlete or a political leader is guilty of a moral lapse (and I hasten to say that the media would never use a word like *guilty* in their news story): "I made a poor choice." Our metaphors or the adjectives we associate with them tell a very great deal about what we really believe. One of our currently popular phrases is "What happened was unfortunate." This is quite different from the idea of sin as a corpse to be carried. If Paul had used metaphors or their accompanying adjectives in such fashion, where we say, "I made a poor choice," Paul at the least would have said, "I played the fool." His metaphor would sting.

At this point someone wants to interrupt me. You want to tell me that Paul had a very poor opinion of himself and that if he were as enlightened as we are he would think better of himself. I submit that quite the opposite is true. Paul had such a high opinion of his potential that he was appalled by his shortcomings. He couldn't imagine lolling along with an eight-minute mile or not even bothering to finish a race when his coach had told him that he could break the four-minute barrier if only he would discipline himself to it.

I believe my analogy is close to the point of Paul's experience. His struggle with sin was not so much at the level of measurable moral failures or abusive habits. His great shame is that he was not living up to his potential. Spiritually speaking, he was capable of breaking the four-minute mile. With his heritage, the influences of his upbringing, his training with Gamaliel, he knew that he should not be spending his life in the lowlands of temptation. How could he waste so much of his soul-energy in thoughts of lust or revenge or petty irritation, when he was capable of the highlands of life? Why waste himself envying Peter or Apollos when his only real competition was Paul? The Paul he knew should become the Paul God wanted him to be.

Paul was no self-hater; he was a person who had caught the vision of his own potential and was sorely distressed that he hadn't yet reached it. Paul was a spiritual violinist, an Itzhak Perlman troubled by a vibration of the string that no one else hears. Paul was an Olympian of the soul who knew that one awkward stride was unworthy of the race. He knew the potential of his soul, and he was repulsed at the idea of anything less. How could he endure this "dead corpse" of mediocre godliness?

But where did Paul get such extravagant ideas of the kind of person he might become? What made him think so highly of his spiritual potential? Surely it began in the Judaism in which he had been raised. He knew the commandment in Leviticus 19:1-2: "The LORD said to Moses, Say to the whole community of the Israelites: You must be holy, because I, the LORD your God, am holy." Holiness was not simply recommended, it was commanded, and Paul took this seriously. No doubt this soul-orientation played a part in his early desire to be a Pharisee.

Then, add to that Paul's experience in Christ. He believed that Christ had "grabbed hold" of him for a purpose, and he was resolved to fulfill that purpose (Philippians 3:12). Paul had a deep understanding of the cross; more compelling, it appears, than that of any other New Testament writer. He saw the redemptive power of the cross and insisted that the cross did what the Law of Moses could not do. For a Christian to live in such a way as to discredit the power of the cross was a kind of living blasphemy. To honor the cross meant that one lives in a way that is consistent with the quality of grace and power implied in the suffering and death of our Lord.

But it isn't easy. Truly godly living is not for the faint of heart. And the higher one sets the bar, the worse one appears when failing. Stan Key, a twenty-first-century Christian, notes that he knows that God empowers with daily strength within, but there is the reality that he has "the will, but not the might." "I am a walking civil war," he cries. Paul would understand Key's metaphor. And Paul would applaud his conclusion, that he will never

28

close the gap between his goal and his struggles until he realizes that the secret is "More of [Christ] and less of me."[4]

As I said earlier, our generation generally avoids using the word *sin*, but when we do, we generally restrict the word to only the most reprehensible conduct; that is, conduct that we can't imagine doing ourselves. Sin is much more sophisticated and much more complicated than that; this is what Jesus was saying when he declared that if we hate our siblings we're murderers, and if we cherish lust in our hearts, we're guilty of adultery. So it is that sin becomes most dangerous when it pulls on the garment of righteousness. *Self*-righteousness, that is. When the earnest, striving Christian pulls out a small plum of achievement and declares, "What a remarkable fellow am I," he not only is taken in by sin but also embraces it with a satisfied smile.

The ultimate goal of the believer is to live up to our name; that is, to become Christlike. In such a pursuit we are always blessed and always challenged. We discover a fullness of life that is beyond description, but as we reach for it we find that what we saw was only the beginning. We realize that nothing matters as much as being all that Christ wants us to be. And if sin keeps us from fulfilling that calling, it is indeed like a dead corpse, burdening the pilgrim soul in the eternal journey.

Vessels in the King's House

Those of us who have lived most or all of our lives in a democracy think that everyone is created equal, and we expect to be treated that way. But our political idealism and the facts of daily life don't always agree. We may all be equal before God, but we aren't all equal in the job market: some are owners, some are supervisors, and some do as they're told. So too in the world of politics: some are elected and some are defeated; some give primary orders, others receive those orders and pass them down to still others, and some people fulfill the orders others give them. This is true even in the world of sports. Some play the game, others are assistant coaches, and at the top are head coaches. Well, not necessarily at the top; in professional sports there are those who own the teams, and while almost no one ever cheers their names, they decide what names will be around to receive the cheers.

I think many of us think that things will of course be better in the kingdom of heaven. The figure of speech should disabuse us of such an idea. When a system is referred to as a *kingdom*, it's clear that somewhere there's a king, and where there's a king, there are orders of responsibility and perhaps even of reward.

Nevertheless, this king language doesn't bother us much because the kings we know about are either figureheads or historical figures. We enjoy reading about England's royalty because it seems to us to be mostly pomp and circumstance. Sometimes we even feel defensive for the Queen and her family when the British press seems to mistreat them. So when we pray, "Thy kingdom come," the words slip past our lips as familiar poetry, with little thought of what it's like to live under absolute authority.

Besides, the kingdom of heaven is different from any other kingdom. It's a sort of kingdom-if-you-want-it idea. The kingdom won't happen to our world except as those who believe in it are effective enough in their prayers and their daily living to bring it to pass. As for its coming in our individual lives—well, that's the anomaly in the kingdom of God. We have a choice as to whether or not we want God's kingdom to set up headquarters in our personal lives. This personal kingdom happens only when you or I choose to let the King come in. We have to step off the throne of self and ask Christ to take the throne. This figure of speech describes what it means to be a Christian: we've given up the throne of our lives to Christ.

At our idealistic best and in our times of profound spiritual dedication, this is beautiful. When I encounter it in biographies or journals of Christianity's greatest souls, I cherish the idea of being such a person. But in the details of daily living, it can be a rather different matter.

Paul makes the point by way of history's most daily of human instruments, the vase or jar or basin. I've always been fascinated with the role vases play in archaeological digs. These containers were the most essential factor in daily living in the ancient world; thus pottery artifacts are the most plentiful record of where and how our ancestors lived. If there was to be water without going to a creek or pond or brook, there had to be a vessel in which it could be transported and stored. If there was to be food for more than one day at a time, there had to be containers where the food could be stored. Pottery is the most basic instrument for dating archaeological periods.

Because we humans are by nature creators and artists, our ancestors began to invest some pots with imagination and beauty so that they were more than utilitarian vehicles; they were also objects of art, by shape, design, or ornamentation. In time, potters began to decorate their pottery with symbols or paintings of their gods and heroes.

Thus as life gained refinement, the pottery developed from instruments of necessity to objects of proud display. The poorest person could have pottery—probably homemade—to store water or food, and the richest could collect pottery of distinction. This principle continues to our time in the distinction we make between daily tableware and the settings we save for special occasions. In a measure, this principle of distinction even operates in our throwaway culture: it ranges from the plastic tableware of the fast-food place to the type people use in outdoor, celebrative occasions where the more economical or the more green-conscious among us wonder if it's right to throw it away.

When Paul wanted a parable for life in the king's household, he turned to their familiar world of pottery. He wasn't the first to do so. Centuries earlier, God instructed the prophet Jeremiah to go to a potter's house. There the prophet watched while a piece of pottery was flawed in the process of shaping, so the potter started on another "as seemed best to him." And God said to Jeremiah, "House of Israel, can't I deal with you like this potter?" (Jeremiah 18:4-6).

Paul picked up on Jeremiah's theme to explain to the Christians at Rome how God had worked with the Jews and was now working with the Gentiles who were becoming a growing influence in the church. The Jews were a minor part of the Roman Empire, both in numbers and in influence. But in God's plan, Paul explained, the Jews had a key place. And they had it not by merit, but by choice; God had chosen the Jew, beginning with Abraham and Sarah. Their son Isaac was chosen to be the carrier of blessing, and of Isaac and Rebecca's twins, the chosen one was Jacob, later to be renamed Israel. And they had these roles because God had chosen them, not because of any apparent qualification on their part.

Paul anticipates his readers' response. "Isn't this unfair on God's part?" And Paul answers their rhetorical question, "Absolutely not!" (Romans 9:14). He continues, "Who do you think you are to talk back to God?" (Romans 9:20). Now Paul goes back to the prophet Isaiah: *"Does the clay say to the potter, 'Why did you make me like this?'"* (Romans 9:20; Isaiah 29:16; 45:9). Since when does the clay talk back to the potter or give instructions regarding the kind of vessel he expects to be?

When Paul writes to the Roman Christians about the potter and the clay, his primary concern is with the role of the Jewish people in the plan of God and then the role of Gentiles. But as Paul makes his point he also gets personal. Perhaps it's because he anticipates his readers' reactions. After all, God's choice of Isaac meant rejection of his brother Ishmael, and God's choosing Jacob meant a secondary place for Jacob's brother Esau. So what does that mean for me, the reader asks; am I a Jacob or an Esau? And Paul answers, "It's really none of your business. You're the clay, not the potter."

Back to the king's household because the king is the one who places the order with the potter. Even the potter is only the artisan, working at the request or the tastes of the buyer. So the potter makes "one pot for special purposes and another for garbage" (Romans 9:21). As Eugene Peterson puts it, "Isn't it obvious that a potter has a perfect right to shape one lump of clay into a vase for holding flowers and another into a pot for cooking beans?"[1]

The answer, it seems to me, is to remember that any role in the king's household is a privilege. This is not an unqualified fact with an earthly king, but if the King be God or our Lord Christ, and the household the kingdom of heaven, then any role is an honor. Further, we trust the judgment of the King; we believe that the King knows better than we do where our best talents lie. It is not that the King loves someone else more than me; indeed, perhaps the most-loving thing the King can do with my qualifications is to let me be the garbage pot, which I will do well, rather than to allow me to serve very poorly and to my shame as a "pot for special purposes." The King shows his love for us by placing us where we can perform most effectively.

We accept this principle in many areas of life. The football coach selects a particular player to carry the ball, a role in which he sometimes gets to cross the goal line with the winning touchdown, to the cheers of the crowd. The coach chooses another person to be a lineman, where he grovels in the mud so the running back can get applause. Is this because the coach hates the lineman? Quite the contrary. I was privileged years ago to enjoy the friendship of a man who always led the ticket in his state's statewide offices. It made no difference which political party was in power, he led everyone. As our friendship became close, I dared ask him why he didn't run for governor. He answered without hesitation that he knew where his skills lay and that he much preferred succeeding in a secondary task to failing in the lead role. I love vocal music. I've learned that some are magnificent in a male quartet who should never be invited to sing a solo.

I remind myself too that there is a price to be paid for being select pottery. The Scriptures tell us that God provided for both Ishmael and Esau and their immediate descendants. They were not key players in the Kingdom, but neither were they outcasts. If I had been from the line of Esau, however, I might have been thankful that I was not an Israelite. God expected so much more of Israel! No one asks the kitchen pot to be beautiful, but the pottery in the King's drawing room is another matter.

I approach this subject with care. In my understanding of Scripture, every believer is part of God's kingdom, and we all have our place. Each of us, that is, is a vase in the King's house. Over a long lifetime I have been privileged to serve as a pastor, a guest preacher, a writer, a teacher, and an administrator. I have worked hard at these tasks and have tried to be faithful, but I have also been rewarded. On the whole, people have treated me with extraordinary kindness. Most of us preachers enjoy side benefits in our work far beyond the material benefits. We receive courtesies that we haven't solicited or measurably deserved. This is not so with some of my spiritual kin in several parts of the world; they serve Christ in danger of imprisonment or martyrdom. I occasionally know some mild mistreatment but no more than a table server is likely to know in any day's work. The psalmist said, "The boundary lines have fallen for me in pleasant places" (Psalm 16:6 NRSV); I could easily claim that as my personal testimony.

So I have to ask, "Why me?" Why should I be a vase on display rather than a pot for the collection of garbage? I don't know. I'm quite sure that heaven will equalize matters in some fashion and that those who have suffered so much in hard places for Christ will enjoy eternal benefits beyond mine. The only word I can speak in my behalf is that I have been as happy when used as a garbage pail as when adorned for display. Somewhere, thank God, I got my theology right: I know that it is enough to be a vessel in the King's house; all else is incidental if only I can serve the King.

But there's a flaw of sorts in Paul's metaphor and in Isaiah's and Jeremiah's before him. I dare to mention it because it's a preacher flaw, and because I too am a preacher, I think I understand it. Paul and the prophets before him told Israel that they were clay and that as such they had no right to talk back to the potter. Remember how emphatic Paul was? "Who do you think you are to talk back to God?" (Romans 9:20). Paul was telling the people how they *ought* to feel and act; this is part of the preacher's assignment. And Paul is right. We humans are clay, and clay isn't supposed to resist the potter. But here's the rub. We humans are a special kind of clay. We *can* talk back to the Potter, and we *do*. It is arrogant of us to do so—almost blasphemous, in fact. But ironically, God made us humans of this kind of clay. God made us of clay that has a mind of its own, and we have a vigorous propensity for showing it.

Nevertheless, the Potter has the final word. When Israel was rebellious clay, the prophets warned them, and still they resisted, until finally the Potter had to do what potters are supposed to do: break up the clay and start over again. This is the potter's right because the potter knows what he hopes to achieve, and the clay doesn't.

That's a problem we clay-folks have. I was struck by it not long ago when I was visiting the Taft Museum in Cincinnati. I came upon an exquisite little work of pottery, a salt cellar, dated 1555. The explanatory line said, "The care lavished on the design and making of this object contrasts with the modest function as a holder of table salt." If physical clay could talk back in the fashion of human-clay, no doubt the salt cellar would have appealed for a more notable function, never dreaming that almost five centuries later it would have a place in an art museum several thousand miles from the place where it was made, and visitors to the museum would pause to look, and look again, then say, "Beautiful! Absolutely beautiful!"

And of course the sixteenth-century human potter would have been almost as surprised as the clay if someone had predicted such a future for his or her salt cellar. Not so with God the Potter, and this is why Paul—like Isaiah and Jeremiah—is impatient with those who resent or mistrust God's intentions.

As we read Paul's letters and listen to his sermons in the Book of Acts, we sometimes realize that Paul (like many of us preachers) is preaching to himself as much as to his hearers. That mood slips through in Paul's Second Letter to the Corinthians. After making a defense of himself and his ministry (as he seemed often to do with the Corinthians), he explained how he felt about his work: "But we have this treasure in clay pots so that the awesome power belongs to God and doesn't come from us" (2 Corinthians 4:7). Paul sees himself and all God's workers not as ornate salt cellars or as hallway ornaments but as *clay pots*. The glory is not in the container but in what the container is privileged to carry.

The early Methodists were a hardy lot. John Wesley intended for them to continue in such a spirit. He adapted a prayer for their use on covenant occasions, especially at New Year's time:

> I am no longer my own, but thine.
> Put me to what thou wilt, rank me with
>   whom thou wilt.
> Put me to doing, put me to suffering.
> Let me be employed by thee or laid aside
>   for thee,
> exalted for thee or brought low for thee.
> Let me be full, let me be empty.
> Let me have all things, let me have
>   nothing.
> I freely and heartily yield all things
> to thy pleasure and disposal.
> And now, O glorious and blessed God,
> Father, Son, and Holy Spirit,
> thou art mine, and I am thine. So be it.
> And the covenant which I have made on
>   earth,
> let it be ratified in heaven. Amen.[2]

If we pray that too easily, we have not prayed it well. It is a prayer for vessels in the King's house, vessels who have learned that it is equally good to be a garbage pot or an artwork in a drawing-room display, if only in so serving we please the King.

The Christian's Larger Family

When I first began thinking about Paul and parables, I smiled to myself as I thought of Jesus' wonderful parable of the father and his two sons in Luke 15, and I tried to imagine Paul saying, "A certain man had two sons" (Luke 15:11). It just didn't sound like Paul. It's not only that Paul didn't seem to be a storyteller but also that he never made references to his biological family. Paul was so personally transparent in his letters, so ready to tell the story of his conversion or to reveal his tension with other church leaders, and so unhesitating in sharing the struggles of his soul, yet he never mentioned his father or mother or siblings. We learn through the Book of Acts that he had a sister and a nephew, when the nephew played a key part in Paul's escape from persecutors (Acts 23:16), but we know nothing more about his biological family—parents, siblings, whatever.

He surely had reason to think well of his parents. Among his credentials, Paul noted with obvious pride that he was from the tribe of Benjamin. It's surely significant that his parents named him Saul, thus recognizing the most notable member of the tribe, King Saul. We judge that Paul's family had some significant public standing by the fact that Paul noted that he was a Roman citizen by birth (Acts 22:28). His parents must have had both financial substance and taste, as demonstrated by Paul's studying under Gamaliel, one of the finest Jewish teachers of the time. Nevertheless, Paul makes no explicit reference to his mother or father.

And of course we know nothing about whether Paul ever married. Scholars and casual students alike have speculated over the centuries, but no one has offered a really convincing case for his having married. If he did, he kept the matter hidden by his not mentioning it.

But in the world of metaphor, Paul had a family. He had brothers and sisters, a mother and sons and an idyllic image of a bride. And in one of his metaphors, Paul had a fatherly image for God that for poignancy and warmth can be placed alongside the loving father in the story of the "certain man [who] had two sons."

Let's begin there. When Paul wants to assure the Christians at Rome that they are fully accepted by God, he writes, "You didn't receive a spirit of slavery to lead you back again into fear, but you received a Spirit that shows you are adopted as his children. With this Spirit, we cry, 'Abba, Father'" (Romans 8:15). The Gentile believers might naturally have felt that they had only secondary rights with God because of God's centuries-long relationship with the Jews. But Paul tells them that they have been *adopted* into God's family. This was a powerful legal term in the first-century world because under Roman law an adopted child was a full and complete member of the family.

If, for instance, a son was adopted before a family had a son by natural birth, the adopted son was still seen legally as the eldest son, with all attendant rights and privileges.

That was the legal understanding. But what of our emotional instinct? Paul writes that through the Spirit, we adopted children cry, "Abba, Father." He uses both the Aramaic and Greek words: *Abba*, from the familiar daily Aramaic speech, and *father*, which is a translation from the Greek word. *Abba* is the word that gives us pause because it was the intimate form of address within the family—much as one might today say Daddy, Papa, or Pops. It's a term you still hear today in the homes, streets, and marketplaces of the Middle East. This is the term Paul uses when he wants his readers in Rome to understand that they are fully accepted by God. It is an embracing, affectionate term.

Paul uses this intimate term again when he's writing to the Christians in Galatia. In this vigorous letter, Paul is angry that false teachers have persuaded some believers to think that Christ's work at Calvary is not enough to guarantee their salvation and that they must also become obedient to the Hebrew Law. Not so, Paul insists: "Because you are sons and daughters, God sent the Spirit of his Son into our hearts, crying, 'Abba, Father!'" (Galatians 4:6). Again, Paul uses both the Aramaic and Greek words for the parent-child relationship, with an emphasis on the everyday, family word, *Abba*.

Scholars in the biblical languages remind us that *Abba* was often the first word a child learned. Yet, adults might continue to use it in speaking to their fathers, regardless of age. And though the Jews referred to God as a heavenly Father, they considered *Abba* as too familiar to use in referring to God.[1]

Thus it is significant that Paul, raised in strict Judaism with its emphasis on careful use of the name of God, would use the most intimate family word as his metaphor for God and that he would do so in these two instances where he is trying most emphatically to assure Christians of their relationship to God. I suppose that a child psychologist might explain Paul's use of *Abba* in one of two ways: for one, that Paul's relationship to his biological father was so beautiful that he quite naturally transferred this term to his relationship to God; or conversely, because Paul lacked a close tie to his biological father he concentrated more than ever on his heavenly father. Whatever may have been the case, Paul used a metaphor from family relationships to convey the warmth and comfort of our relationship with Almighty God. John Knox, the mid-twentieth-century New Testament scholar, noted that Paul knew Aramaic in its daily use and "that it may well have been the language of his prayers."[2]

Whether or not Paul used the term in his prayers, it is clear that, when Paul uses *Abba* as his name for God, he is in the spirit of Jesus' parable. When the father in Jesus' parable runs to meet his vagabond son, embracing him and welcoming him back into the family, it is an "Abba" moment. The boy said, "I no longer deserve to be called your son," but the father interrupted, "This son of mine was dead and has come back to life!" (Luke 15:21, 24). There's an *Abba* intimacy in that grand welcome. William Barclay declares, "There is no one single letter that he ever wrote in which Paul does not call God *Father*."[3] This is impressive, indeed. But the language takes on new depth and pathos when Paul tells believers that God is *Abba* Father.

When we speak of God as Father, we enter the possibility of an extended metaphor. Paul does just that. If you and I are adopted as daughters and sons of God, it follows that we have a special relationship to Jesus Christ because he is the Son of God. So Paul reasons, "We are God's heirs and *fellow heirs with*

Christ, if we really suffer with him so that we can also be glorified with him" (Romans 8:17, italics mine). Thus, Jesus Christ, God's Son "would be the first of many brothers and sisters" (Romans 8:29). Paul sees the community of believers as a family: God is the Father, Christ the elder brother, with the rest of us among "many brothers and sisters."

With this theological background in mind, it isn't surprising that Paul makes so much of the language of family in referring to his fellow believers. We are not simply members of the same organization, or subscribers to the same doctrinal or political positions, we are *family;* we are brothers and sisters. By salvation we have been adopted into the one great family with the same divine Father.

Paul uses this family metaphor constantly, especially in the greetings with which he concludes many letters (for example, 1 Corinthians 16:20; 2 Corinthians 13:11; Galatians 6:18). There must have been many reasons why the early believers saw themselves as brothers and sisters. For one, they recognized their spiritual heritage in the Hebrew Scriptures in the family of Abraham and then, more particularly, in the descendants of Israel. For the Jews, the bond was biological; for the church, made up increasingly of people from many ethnic and racial groups, the bond was spiritual. But they knew beyond all question that they were the children of God and co-heirs with Jesus Christ.

There's no doubt that there was a further psychological bonding among Christians, in their being a small, persecuted body. Often the powers of the government were against them, and so were the other religions. With only the least provocation, communities and whole governments could organize to oppress them. Under such circumstances, Christians came to feel that all they had in this world was each other. In many instances, believers had been alienated from their families by becoming Christians, which made their fellow believers their new family. And because of the threats under which they lived, it became an especially close-knit family. If you belonged, you belonged all the way.

It was natural, then, for further family language to become part of the Christian metaphor. So in Paul's greetings to believers in Rome, he writes, "Greet Rufus, chosen in the Lord; and greet his mother—a mother to me also" (Romans 16:13 NRSV). We wish Paul had filled out that greeting with details, but they're left to our imagination. For Paul and all of the traveling Christian prophets, evangelists, and teachers, if they had any home it was through the hospitality that local Christians offered. Here there would be food—meager, perhaps, but shared so gladly that it was gourmet in spirit. Here there was an extra pallet on which to sleep, perhaps a corner where Paul could read.

But most of all, there was the caring. This, one cannot buy and cannot legislate. It is a matter of the heart. Etiquette may provide a vocabulary, but love puts emotional content into the words. Paul and one or two of his companions arrive in a community, weary from the road, always wondering when the law might apprehend them on some trumped-up charge, probably having eaten no hot food in several days, and then a "mother" greets them. Here there is lodging and food. And with it the kind of chiding that is part of the greeting: "You haven't been taking care of yourself, have you! You need a good bath. How long since you've had a full meal? Didn't those people in Corinth know enough to pack some food for you?" I hear it all when Paul writes, "Greet Rufus's mother—a mother to me also." I think I see Paul smiling as he dictates that line. Perhaps Paul remembers a line from the great battle song in the Book of Judges that exulted how Deborah "arose as a mother in Israel" (Judges 5:7). The church is now the new Israel, and Paul has found a new mother in Israel, a different kind of Deborah.

Paul extends the family metaphor with particular vigor when he asserts his role as a father in the faith. So he tells the people at Corinth when he sends young Timothy to them, "He's my loved and trusted child in the Lord" (1 Corinthians 4:17). In the letters addressed to Timothy, Timothy is Paul's "true child in the faith" (1 Timothy 1:2) and "my dear child" (2 Timothy 1:2). Titus is "my true child in a common faith" (Titus 1:4). Paul may have used this language in the sense that Timothy and Titus came to their faith through him; that is, they were his converts. In the case of Timothy, however, Paul seems to credit Timothy's mother and grandmother, Eunice and Lois, for his place in Christ, with Paul's special role coming later in his laying hands on Timothy for the anointing and gifts of the Spirit (2 Timothy 1:5-6). It seems likely, therefore, that at least in Timothy's case, Paul saw his role as the older and more experienced gospel worker who stood ready at all times to watch over their ministry.

The other person that Paul identifies specifically as his child or son in the faith is a very special case, Onesimus, the runaway slave. It seems that he and Onesimus met in prison. If one were locked up with Paul, the odds were high that one would know Christ as Lord before many moons had passed. So it was with Onesimus. When Paul sends him back to his master, Philemon, it is with a letter of appeal on Onesimus' behalf. It is a letter of particular affection for both Philemon and Onesimus. In it Paul writes, "I, Paul…appeal to you for my child Onesimus. I became his father in the faith during my time in prison" (Philemon 9-10).

It is almost beyond question that Paul never had biological children, but he took great pride in his spiritual children—many of whom, like Philemon, came to their faith directly under his influence and ministry and still others like Timothy, Titus, Silas, Luke, Epaphroditus, Lydia, Priscilla, Aquila—where would the list begin or end of those persons whose birth in Christ might directly or indirectly relate to Paul, and whose growth and direction in faith and ministry bore Paul's influence and image?

Paul was familiar enough with Greek mythology that he might easily have seen himself as a mentor to his converts and followers. And he was himself debtor enough to his great teacher, Gamaliel, that he could proudly have identified himself as the teacher, the rabbi, for the persons who looked to him for knowledge, wisdom, and daily guidance. But his favorite term for those who knew him best was in the metaphor of father and child.

Indeed, the concept was so dear to him that he was ready also to bear its pain and disappointments. Parenthood is not an unscarred title; to be a parent is to accept the burden of worry and sometimes of disappointment and sorrow. Paul accepts the full meaning of parenthood when he writes to his faltering followers in Galatia, "My little children, I am going through labor pains again until Christ is formed in you" (Galatians 4:19). Paul's first-century world felt that birth pangs were the most severe pain humans might suffer. You might want to tell Paul that labor pains belong to women, not men, but it is in this very daring, confused metaphor that we see just how deeply Paul felt about his family relationship to fellow believers in general and to his own children in the faith in particular. The apostle couldn't be more eloquent in describing his sense of the family of God than when he dares to claim birth pangs, a pain beyond his male experience.

Paul's family metaphors continue to this present day. I sense, however, that they are not as strong as they were a generation or two ago. I grew up in two worlds: a secular world where adults were known as Mister or Missus, or perhaps Doctor, and a church world where everyone was either Brother or Sister. Today it is only in some smaller religious bodies that a fellow believer is so addressed. Nor is the concept of family as strong as it was. We're more likely to find that term on the sports page, where athletes say of their teammates, "We're a family." I honor their use of the word, and I think I understand it. When you've worked hard for a common goal and have won and lost together, you are bonded in a special way. But I'm a bit sad that the language seems to belong more to the locker room than to the church.

I'm sure it was easier for church members to feel their family ties when communities were smaller, so that people belonged in the village church, or in neighborhood churches in a city. Now people live in one community or city, work in another, shop in a third, and worship in still another. It is not like the revered country church where members knew one another through generations and saw their biological families buried in a cemetery adjoining the church building.

Yet having recognized that times have changed, and that automobiles, commerce, school systems, iPhones, and social media have virtually revolutionized human relationships, I nevertheless wonder if we have lost something in the church. Is there a family-sense in the church that should make terms like brother, sister, and father-mother-son-daughter in the faith meaningful and cherished language? Language matters, you know, and when we lose words, we lose the realities that go with the words. And conversely—and this may be our problem—when we lose realities, we no longer have need for the words.

As for Paul and his metaphor, he had a family. We know little or nothing about his father and mother, he probably had no wife and certainly no physical children, but he had family. It's no wonder that he worked the metaphor so hard and so broadly when the reality was so real and so beautiful.

Babies and Grown-ups Too

O ne night an unlikely visitor came, unannounced, to talk
with Jesus. He was a person of reputation, of significant
education and intelligence, and a person of recognized leadership within the Jewish community.

He was putting all of this standing in danger when he came
to see Jesus. True, Jesus was very popular, and sought out by
growing crowds, but the crowds were common folks, who were
needy in every way. They had little or nothing to lose by associating with the teacher from the hill country of Nazareth. But if
Nicodemus were seen associating with Jesus—and particularly,
seeking counsel from him—his role in the Jewish community in
general and especially within its leadership would suffer badly,
perhaps irreparably.

Nevertheless, Nicodemus came to see Jesus. He approached
Jesus with utmost courtesy, addressing him as a rabbi and as one
sent from God. "Rabbi, we know that you are a teacher who
has come from God, for no one could do these miraculous signs

that you do unless God is with him" (John 3:2). Jesus answered abruptly, brushing aside Nicodemus's graciousness without even a word of thanks. Imagine a twenty-first-century person of position greeting a doctor, "I've come to you because you are one of the finest heart specialists in the western world," and the doctor replying without a preliminary word, "If you don't lose some weight, you'll be dead in six months." Such was the quality of Jesus' reply: "I assure you, unless someone is born anew, it's not possible to see God's kingdom" (John 3:3). Jesus sensed that Nicodemus was looking for the kingdom of God, and he cut to the chase without any customary formalities.

The conversation that followed is one of the most significant in all of the New Testament and basic to any serious study of Christian doctrine. It announces that God's kingdom is not an organization one chooses to join, not a philosophy one espouses, and not an achievement won by study and preparation. Nor is it something of a privilege into which one is born, by right of family line. It is a status that one gets by birth, a *second* birth, an entirely new life.

This is a powerful metaphor, and if it hadn't been tamed for us by rather common usage, we probably would respond the way Nicodemus did. "How is it possible for an adult to be born? It's impossible to enter the mother's womb for a second time and be born, isn't it?" (John 3:4). I don't think Nicodemus was so intellectually dull that he thought Jesus was talking about a physical experience. Nicodemus was, however, a person who had sought passionately and unsuccessfully for fullness of life in God; this was why he was putting his social and religious status in jeopardy by coming to the rabbi from Nazareth. Thus he answered Jesus with a heart cry because he knew by experience how nearly impossible it is to start over when you're middle-aged. (Or twenty-five, for that matter.) How can one become a new person after years of becoming the kind of person you are; after years of experiences good and bad, of striving, of failures and faux-successes, of wanting to be better but never making it? That is, it's too late to go back to your mother's womb, and it seems quite as impossible.

Jesus answered by reiterating what he had already said but adding an explanatory phrase or two. "I assure you, unless someone is born of water and the Spirit, it's not possible to enter God's kingdom. Whatever is born of the flesh is flesh, and whatever is born of the Spirit is spirit" (John 3:5-6). All of us have been born of the flesh; that's how we got here. But God has willed that we should also be born of the Spirit, and it is this being born of the Spirit—that is, born anew, born a second time, born again—that brings us into the kingdom of God.

There are many ways to describe entry into the Christian life and perhaps almost as many metaphors as the number of preachers, poets, teachers, and storytellers employing them. But ultimately our personal Christian faith comes down to this, that we need a radical change; and there's no better way to describe this change than to speak of a new birth. We human creatures are born of flesh like earth's other creatures. But we're different in that the breath of God is in us, as the creation story declares (Genesis 2:7). Thus we never fulfill our divinely ordained potential and our own deepest longings unless we are born anew by a further action of God's Spirit, another invasion by the breath of God. A human who has been born only of the flesh is unfinished; we are meant also to be born of the Spirit of God.

"Born again" is a powerful metaphor. It isn't the only powerful one, by any means. Jesus gave another in the language of lostness, the lost sheep and the lost coin in Luke 15. And in that same chapter, the language of returning home, in the story of the prodigal. And still another when he told of a merchant who sold everything he had in order to get a pearl that was without price (Matthew 13:45-46).

But the particular power of the "born again" picture is that it makes clear that becoming a Christian is not just an event or an experience or a decision, wonderful and memorable as these may be; it is a way of *life*. It is not an end but a beginning. Great as a birth is, it is not complete in itself; it is only the initial step toward completeness.

The apostle Paul knew as much. It isn't surprising that he picked up Jesus' metaphor in his letters to his converts. More important, he developed the metaphor. Paul, the pastor and teacher, knew that conversion, no matter how miraculous, is only the beginning. His own conversion near Damascus is a model for spectacular religious experience, but the drama was followed by a key sentence: "Now get up and enter the city. You will be told what you must do" (Acts 9:6). Only rarely does a new convert receive the kind of specifics that Ananias no doubt passed on to Paul: "This man is the agent I have chosen to carry my name before Gentiles, kings, and Israelites" (Acts 9:15). But every convert has the basic order that comes with the experience of birth; that is, the purpose of being born is to grow up. Birth is not an end in itself; it matters because it is the earthly start of a new life.

Though Paul was not a physical parent he obviously honored the role. We saw this in the figures of speech Paul used, as indicated in our previous chapter. He becomes even more specific when he discusses the fragility of young Christians and their need for special care. He could have exercised authority in his dealings with his followers, he told the Thessalonians, but "we were gentle with you like a nursing mother caring for her own children" (1 Thessalonians 2:7). It was somewhat common among the Romans, especially the more wealthy, to employ a wet nurse for their infants, but even some secular philosophers felt that in such an arrangement the child missed the mother's love. When Paul portrays his care for his converts by the image of a nursing mother, he has a very convincing picture of the feeling he has for his people, and with that metaphor he builds on the image of the new Christian as an infant in the faith: that is, as someone who has been "born anew" into faith.

Paul holds to that image when he writes to the Corinthians, but this time his metaphor carries rebuke. An emphatic one, in fact. He tells the people that they shouldn't be such babies; it's time they grew up. "Brothers and sisters, I couldn't talk to you like spiritual people but like unspiritual people, like babies in Christ. I gave you milk to drink instead of solid food, because you weren't up to it yet" (1 Corinthians 3:1-2). New Christians are babies, fresh from the womb of faith, and those who care for them should feed them accordingly; they are physically constituted for nourishment by milk. But they need at some point to move from the infant diet to that of a growing child, or their physical development will suffer. And so it is, Paul wants us to know, in the spiritual life. Spiritual infants need, in time, to move to the diet of a healthy child, and then of a young adult, and on into a mature Christian life.

Sociologists who specialize in religious studies note that the American church population is growing increasingly older. Many congregations have a median age of sixty years or older. As some clergy look at these figures (and sometimes at their own congregations), they say that they don't want to be a chaplain in a hospice; they want, rather, to evangelize a younger generation rather than presiding over people who can be expected to die within a few years.

I'm troubled by such statements because I honor chaplains in any age group, and I think their role is especially important for their ministry to those who are reaching the end of life on this planet. But I'm especially uneasy with such an outlook because I have seen so much evangelism of one kind or another that is excited about bringing persons to birth but that has failed to lead those persons to mature, exemplary faith. As a result, vast numbers join churches, are confirmed, or come to decision in evangelistic programs and within a few months or years are nowhere to be seen. They have gotten just enough religion to know a spiritual birth of one kind or another, but from lack of food they have died. Thus I make a double indictment: the church that never brings souls to birth is failing its mission. So is the church that announces new births but that never gets its converts past a milk diet. Being born again is the beginning of the story, not its end. The goal of the new birth is that we grow up to become mature believers, examples to a culture that seldom sees Christianity at its adult best.

This is the issue that concerned Paul. It must have been a particularly challenging issue for the first generation of believers. The level of zeal was high. There was a holy excitement wherever the apostles, prophets, and evangelists preached. They seemed, indeed, to be "turning the world upside down." But often people like Paul stayed in a community only months or a year or two, then moved on to other places of need. It had to be so if they were to go into all the world with the gospel. But, in the process, there was the danger that converts would have little teaching and little knowledge of doctrine and of the ethical conduct that should characterize the Christian faith.

And this, you see, is what the New Testament epistles are all about. Paul and the other apostolic writers were seeking through the epistles to answer the doctrinal questions that were arising in the churches and address the ethical issues—the issues of everyday conduct—that were so closely related to their life in Christ. Paul wanted his people to grow up. It violated his sense of the purpose of the Christian life when he saw believers who after years in the church were still infants.

It was this passion for mature Christians that made Paul speak so urgently to the believers in Galatia, in the passage I mentioned in the previous chapter. "My little children, I'm going through labor pains again until Christ is formed in you" (Galatians 4:19). Here Paul refers to their having been born again, but something is wrong; so wrong that if it were possible he would go through the pains of childbirth again if only they would emerge as healthy infants, ready to grow into the likeness of Christ.

It would be quite exciting if we could have a daring conversation in our churches at certain key times. For instance, at the end of a series of confirmation classes for young people, or membership training classes for adults, or following a new life mission, when people have publicly confessed their faith in Christ. At such a time, it would be quite right, quite exciting, and probably quite unsettling if the pastor or teacher were to ask, "Now what do you hope to be when you grow up?" That is, we're asking this born-anew person what aim they have for the new life that is in them. What will be the consummation of it all? A similar question could be asked of parents and sponsors in a consultation before or after the baptism of an infant: "What do you want your baby to be when she grows up?" Perhaps then the parents and sponsors would have a more profound sense of the promises made at the altar of baptism.

Paul knew what he expected. He believed it was the ultimate business of the church. He explained that Christ has equipped the church with apostles, prophets, evangelists, pastors, and teachers. Why? "His purpose was to equip God's people for the work of serving and building up the body of Christ." And where will this lead? "Until we all reach the unity of faith and knowledge of God's Son." And what will that be like? "God's goal is for us to become mature adults—to be fully grown, measured by the standard of the fullness of Christ." And with that, Paul returns again to the baby question, the new birth question: "As a result, we aren't supposed to be infants any longer" (Ephesians 4:11-14).

Paul goes on from there to deal with some specific problems the people were facing in the church at Ephesus, problems that might seem very much like those we still face in our cities and villages today; it's just a matter of dressing them in the twenty-first-century clothes. But the point is the same in every generation, every cultural setting, and in all the business of living. If we are to be the salt of the earth, the people bringing redemption to our time and place, we will need to be mature adults. Not by the measure of the calendar, and not by the measure of psychology or pedagogy, though these measures are significant in their own right. Ours is a more demanding measure, more demanding by far: we are "measured by the standard of the fullness of Christ."

That is, if we dared to have a question session for confirmands, new church members, or new believers, persons who have been born again, and were to ask the question, "What do you want to be when you grow up?" we would expect a daring answer: "I want to be like Jesus." So too with the question for the parents and their supporters at a baptismal service: "What do you want this child to be when [he or she] grows up?" The daring answer: "I want [her or him] to be like Jesus."

Isn't this the end of it all? Isn't this the purpose of the church? And isn't this what makes us different from all the other organizations in our communities? Our many admirable community programs seek—often very admirably—to benefit our social fulfillment, our economic security, our intellectual capacity, our cultural hunger, and our desire for entertainment pleasure. The church touches all of these but with a different ultimate goal in mind. We want to become like Jesus. We feel compelled to *grow up*, by the most demanding of all measures, the fullness of Christ. We want to become like Jesus.

Nicodemus was a seeker when he came to Jesus. He was a scholar, a model citizen, an earnest man who wanted a full life, a man who was wise enough to know that there was more to life than he had found. So Jesus gave him a metaphor to challenge him: you need to be born anew.

And Paul picked up the metaphor. He took it seriously. So you've been born again? Now what do you expect to be when you grow up? Because that's the purpose of birth, you know: the aim, at last, is to grow up. To become like Jesus.

Portraits of the Church

The four Gospels, Matthew, Mark, Luke, and John, give us several thousand words of Jesus' teaching but say almost nothing about the church. In fact, only the Gospel of Matthew uses the word and then only on two occasions. The first occurs when Jesus asks the disciples who people say he is, then asks them who they believe him to be. When Simon Peter answers, "You are the Christ, the Son of the living God," Jesus replies, "I'll build my church on this rock" (Matthew 16:13-18). Sometime later when Jesus is telling the disciples how to handle a grievance between believers, he explains how to use the church as part of the adjudicating process (Matthew 18:15-17). Jesus speaks a very great deal about the kingdom of God or the kingdom of heaven; these references apply in some ways to the church but not in a fully synonymous or interchangeable way. The kingdom of God is bigger than the church, and yet it cannot exist without the church.

But the language of faith changes dramatically on the Day of Pentecost. Where the Gospels mention the church only twice, the Acts of the Apostles speak of it repeatedly, and they do so in a natural way that assumes its importance. It's no wonder that we refer to the Day of Pentecost as the birthday of the church because, from that point on, *church* is the dominant term. In the Greek, the word is *ekklesia,* "the called-out ones." The word appears in Acts 2:47, just after the report of the outpouring of the Holy Spirit: "The Lord added daily to the community those who were being saved." Several fine translations use words such as *community* or *number,* then use *church* in the continuing story in the Book of Acts whenever *ekklesia* appears. The King James Version is consistent in its translation. Mind you, the Greek word can be translated several ways, but because the same body of believers is being referred to, it seems right to use the word *church* from the beginning, for obviously a new body had now come into existence. And they were, indeed, "the called-out" ones. Those who affiliated themselves with Christ and the cross were different from all of the culture around them, and they gladly dared to be so.

Paul uses the word some sixty times in his letters, and he more than anyone else tells us what the church is. He does so in the style we've seen to be typical of him: he describes with metaphors. Three of these metaphors are especially helpful to our understanding of what God expects the church to be.

Let me pause momentarily, however, to mention a metaphor we might have expected Paul to use, one that would have seemed natural to him but that he did not develop. Paul's own heritage was with the Jews, who were the nation of God, unlike the "nations [that] rant" and "the leaders [who] scheme together / against the LORD and / against his anointed one" (Psalm 2:1-2). We might expect Paul to take the idea of a nation and to make it his metaphor to describe the new body through whom God's purposes would unfold. He could have pictured believers as God's *new* nation, one made up of Jews and Greeks, male and female, slave and free, and thus a nation very different from the pattern of ethnic peoples. For some reason, however, Paul didn't choose to use this metaphor that would have seemed so compatible with who he was. Instead, he gave us three pictures, each very different from the others.

The metaphor he develops in greatest detail portrays the church as a *body*, a physical, human body. The church at Corinth was very alive, very spiritual, and possessed of very strong opinions. Its members cherished the manifestations of the Holy Spirit, and they became competitive among themselves about these manifestations. Paul set out to let them know that all the spiritual gifts were of God and that one gift was not to be prized above the others, nor was any person to feel exalted because of one particular gift. He made his case by a metaphor of the body: "The human body...is a unit and has many parts; and all the parts of the body are one body, even though there are many" (1 Corinthians 12:12). The foot and the hand or the ear and the eye don't argue about their roles, Paul says, because the body needs them all. Further, "the parts of the body that people think are the weakest are the most necessary" (12:22), and "the private parts of our body that aren't presentable are the ones that are given the most dignity" (12:23).

It is a graphic, convincing argument; its only weakness is in our failure to take it fully to heart. The logic is clear, as Paul says when he uses the same figure of speech in writing to the church at Rome. "We have many parts in one body, but the parts don't all have the same function. In the same way, though there are many of us, we are one body in Christ, and individually we belong to each other" (Romans 12:4-5). When we hurt some part of the body, we are hurting our very selves, the whole body.

No part of the body can suffer without every part being victimized in some measure or other.

The metaphor becomes all the more demanding when we see its strategic tie. This body that we call the church is in fact "the body of Christ" (1 Corinthians 12:12). The hurt we do when we hurt one another injures not only a denomination or doctrinal branch or a certain group of believers or a particular individual. We are doing violence to the body of our Lord. When the church is torn by strife and self-interest, we are dismembering the body of Christ.

Paul could have gotten this concept of the church as the body of Christ at the hour of his conversion. When Paul was confronted on the road to Damascus the voice asked, "Saul, Saul, why are you harassing me?" Paul knew it was the voice of God, so he answered, "Who are you, Lord?" Paul's passion was for God; how possibly, his soul cried, could he be persecuting God? And the voice answered, "I am Jesus, whom you are harassing" (Acts 9:4-5). To persecute the believers was to persecute Jesus, the Christ. No wonder the church, as the body of Christ, was such a dominant vision in Paul's mind. It was far more than a compelling figure of speech; it was part of his very pilgrimage of salvation.

There is also dynamic strength in this picture. God has "put everything under Christ's feet," Paul writes, "and made him head of everything in the church, which is his body. His body, the church, is the fullness of Christ, who fills everything in every way" (Ephesians 1:22-23). If the church is, in fact, "the fullness of Christ," we should have much more confidence in its significance and in its ability to make a difference in our world and an eternal difference, at that. There is much more to us, the church, than appears to the eye or that can be measured by any earthly statistics.

Paul's second picture of the church is not so emotionally charged. It appeals to a quite different part of our thinking. Paul may never have heard of our right-brain, left-brain understanding, but he was enough of a teacher and a logician to realize that different human beings have very different ways of grasping ideas. For those in Paul's hearing who were mathematically or structurally inclined—or for that matter, almost anyone who had ever watched the construction of a great public building (of which there were many in the Roman Empire) or even a simple village home—he had a metaphor they could grasp easily and with satisfaction.

In this instance, Paul chooses once again to mix his metaphors. He begins here by referring to the church as God's household—that is, as a family—and then as a building: "You belong to God's household. As God's household, you are built on the foundation of the apostles and prophets with Christ Jesus himself as the cornerstone. The whole building is joined together in him, and it grows up into a temple that is dedicated to the Lord" (Ephesians 2:19-21).

Notice first that you and I are the church; *we* are God's building. As someone has said, every Christian is a stone in God's house. And see what an honor it is to be part of this building: the foundation is the apostles and prophets, and the cornerstone is none other than our Lord Christ. Let no member of the church think of himself or herself as insignificant; we are part of a structure that includes the saints of the ages and Christ himself. If someone objects that she is hardly a stone— a pebble, perhaps!—let us remind her that no part, however poorly imagined, is inconsequential when it contributes to such an eternal structure.

Paul turns the picture of the building another way when he writes to the people at Corinth. He tells us, "You are . . . God's building" (1 Corinthians 3:9), but then he changes the figures and pictures us as the workers who are raising up the building. Paul says with some pride that he has "laid a foundation like a wise master builder according to God's grace that was given to me" (3:10). But now others are adding to the building, and the apostle wants them to be sure they are building with great care, especially in their choice of materials. The foundation is Jesus Christ, and there can be no other (3:11), but the material that we bring to the building can be "gold, silver, precious stones, wood, grass, or hay" (3:12). The day will come, Paul warns, when the quality of our contribution "will be revealed with fire—the fire will test the quality of each one's work. If anyone's work survives, they'll get a reward. But if anyone's work goes up in flames, they'll lose it. However, they themselves will be saved as if they had gone through a fire" (3:13-15).

For years I tried to be a careful statistician of my work: I knew how many sermons I had preached in a given year, how many pastoral calls I had made, how many persons received into church membership. I hesitated to say how many souls had been saved because only the Holy Spirit can report such a statistic with certainty. But even those matters that can be counted by human reckoning face the test of eternal value. Calls have been made, sermons preached, books written, persons counseled, but to how much eternal accomplishment? And in what spirit was the work done? How often were duties performed in perfunctory fashion or primarily to win human approval? By contrast, how much of the work done had the fragrance of eternity, of grace, and of love? It is a hard question, and each of us needs to raise it regarding our service, our giving, and our religious ceremonies. The church is a building, an eternal building, and each of us needs to ask whether the work we bring to it is eternal "gold, silver, and precious stones" that will stand the fire of God's judgment.

And above all we need to remember that the cornerstone is Jesus Christ. The church, whatever its human identifications and its various affiliations, has its meaning only by way of its cornerstone. Without the cornerstone, the church is like any other human institution—honorable in its intentions, well-meaning in its aims, and admirable in its finest moments but human, and thus its parts will fall into dust. By contrast, the church is God's building, and its cornerstone is Jesus Christ. It is eternal, and we should treat it accordingly.

It's probably presumptuous to choose one of Paul's church metaphors as superior to the others. As I've already indicated, different pictures appeal to different tastes. But the portrait that would be the most appealing to our imagination and probably the most challenging to our daily living is that which pictures us as the bride of Christ.

The general context of this metaphor is not unique to Paul. Jesus worked with the same basic data in the parable of the ten bridesmaids as a picture of the kingdom of heaven (Matthew 25:1-13). The coming of the kingdom is pictured as a wedding, but in Jesus' parable, the emphasis is on the bridesmaids who are supposed to wait faithfully with the bride. The Book of Revelation also works with a wedding theme in its glorious climax in a wedding banquet. Here Christ is described as the Lamb who is also the groom (Revelation 19:1-10).

It isn't surprising that Jesus built a parable around a marriage ceremony and that Revelation brings the divine story to a climax with a wedding feast, nor is it surprising that Paul used such a figure of speech. The metaphor goes all the way back to the Old Testament prophets. Three, in particular, use the image of marriage to describe the relationship of God and the chosen people. Jeremiah declares,

> Surely, as a treacherous wife leaves her
> husband,
> so have you been treacherous to me, O
> house of Israel,
> declares the LORD.
> (Jeremiah 3:20 ESV)

Ezekiel makes a lengthy accusation against Israel and Judah for adultery against the Lord God by following after the gods of other nations (Ezekiel 23). Hosea's message is built upon the marriage of God and Israel and Israel's unfaithfulness. In one of the most moving passages, God pleads with Israel, "And I will betroth you to me forever. I will betroth you to me in righteousness and in justice, in steadfast love and in mercy. I will betroth you to me in faithfulness. And you shall know the LORD" (Hosea 2:19-20 ESV).

Paul was, of course, familiar with the Hebrew Scriptures, including the prophets, and he saw the church as God's new people, the bride anticipated in the call to Abraham centuries before when God told Abraham that through him "all the families of the earth / will be blessed" (Genesis 12:3). God's ultimate vision went beyond Abraham's physical descendants to all the earth. As the apostle to the Gentiles, Paul saw this greater vision coming to pass in his daily mission.

Even though Paul knew through the prophets how Israel had fallen short of God's vision for his people, he maintained high hopes for the church as the bride of Christ. It is in this context that he expressed his disappointment to the people at Corinth. "As your father, I promised you in marriage to one husband. I promised to present you as an innocent virgin to Christ himself" (2 Corinthians 11:2). The late William Barclay reminds us that in a Jewish wedding two persons were known as the friends of the bridegroom. They had several responsibilities but above all to protect the purity of the bride. "So Paul thinks of Christ as the bridegroom, and of himself as the friend of the bridegroom, and of the Church of Corinth as the bride who is being prepared for Christ," Barclay writes; thus Paul's primary responsibility is to "present the Church at Corinth a pure and unspotted bride to Jesus Christ."[1]

But no matter what Paul's disappointments with any particular congregation at any given time, he continued to have high hopes for the church. He judged the church not by her deeds but by God's expectations. This is his mood when he writes to the Ephesians, and it is so dominant in his spirit that it slips into one of his admonitions for daily godly living. As Paul explains how husbands and wives ought to love one another, he notes that Christ gave himself for the church "to make her holy....He did this to present himself with a splendid church, one without any sort of stain or wrinkle on her clothes, but rather one that is holy and blameless" (Ephesians 5:26-27).

Paul had wonderfully high hopes for the church. He had those hopes in spite of disappointments at Thessalonica, at Corinth, in the churches of Galatia, and even in his beloved believers in Philippi. What was Paul's secret? How could he keep so hopeful in the face of "the facts" of his churches? You and I need to know, because we belong to imperfect congregations in the midst of imperfect denominations (or non-denominational churches, which are, of course, their own little denominations). How could Paul dare to see the church as a pure bride, "without any sort of stain or wrinkle on her clothes"?

Quite simply, he continued to see the church as what God intended for her to be and what, therefore, she will by grace become. Only occasionally, perhaps only sometimes momentarily, does the church seem like such a pure bride. But this is what our Lord expects of us, so I'm voting with Paul. I'm expecting us to fulfill God's vision.

The Christian as Soldier and as Actor,

You may feel I'm being playful or unduly clever in the title of this chapter, and perhaps I am. One of these metaphors, soldier and actor, is likely to offend some of you, and still others may be offended by both. I'll confess that I'm pressing things in using the term *actor* as a metaphor; I'll make that case later, and I promise you that it's an important one even if the term itself seems in question.

The Christian as soldier is another matter. There's no question that Paul saw the Christian life as engagement in a continuing conflict, and he used the metaphor effectively. It's also true, however, that many Christians draw back from this metaphor. In their commitment to peace, they avoid any of the language of warfare. I honor their point because I know that language is powerful and that it influences our thinking in ways we don't always recognize.

Nevertheless, the Scriptures tell us that a war is going on in our world. Because this is the case, we'd better know all we can about its nature and our part in it. We gain nothing by avoiding the facts. I was first compelled by these facts something over twenty years ago when I wrote a devotional book, which in the course of a year led its readers through the Bible, from Genesis through Revelation. I slowly began to realize that the Bible is the story of a battle—the war between good and evil. This battle begins in Genesis 3, and it doesn't end until the closing chapters of Revelation. This war won't end until "the kingdom of the world has become / the kingdom of our Lord and his Christ" (Revelation 11:15).

You can trace this struggle between good and evil by high points. It was fought out in Noah's time when all the thoughts and deeds of the culture were evil and the only voice for purity and goodness was that of Noah: "Noah was a moral and exemplary man" (Genesis 6:9). The conflict was present when God brought the Israelite slaves out of Egypt, to make them a different people, a holy nation—and it was there when in their own struggle with evil the people of Israel failed God repeatedly. You see the war between good and evil in the days of the judges and kings of Israel—and again, when the nation that was called to be good didn't always prove to be good, when in fact evil invaded the guardians of goodness. It was at such times that God raised up prophets who fought evil with the most majestic calls to righteousness that still stir the soul twenty-five to thirty centuries later.

Sometimes the battle has taken on peculiar proportions; at times, if you didn't see the names on the back of the uniforms, you wouldn't know for whom to cheer. Sometimes God's most notable figures—men like Abraham and Jacob and David—conducted themselves very much like the people they were supposed to convert. And sometimes pagan kings of pagan nations served God by helping to restore God's chosen people, Israel, after Israel had gone astray.

When the story took its climactic turn in the New Testament with the coming of Jesus, the picture became muddied again. The religious leadership of Israel, God's people, led the way in rejecting Christ. God then cobbled together a group of fishermen, tax collectors, nondescripts, and a tentmaker to take the place of the Levites and to be the leaders of the new Kingdom; we call them the church. But these folks weren't perfect, either. If they had been, we wouldn't have the books of the New Testament that we call the epistles because those books were written primarily to deal with those times when the people of God, the church, weren't acting like the people of God.

We've written this conflict into our liturgy, in language familiar to generations both Catholic and Protestant, that there is the Church Militant and the Church Triumphant. The Church Militant is the body of Christians currently living on the earth, the "Christian militia" engaged in the struggle against "the rulers of the darkness of this world"; the Church Triumphant comprises those who are in heaven. Thus, at funeral services, we sometimes hear the phrase, "our friend has gone from the Church Militant to the Church Triumphant."

All of which is to say that not only are we engaged in a battle between good and evil but also that the battle is very complex. The most complicated factor is this, that the major battleground is the individual human soul. Here is Armageddon, Hastings, Valley Forge, Gettysburg, or the Battle of the Bulge on any day of any week, right in the human soul, yours and mine.

Paul knew this. He knew it from working with his believers in Corinth and Galatia, and he knew it from the struggles of his own soul. And he could find no better way of describing it than in the language of warfare. So he wrote,

> Put on God's armor so that you can make a stand against the tricks of the devil. We aren't fighting against human enemies but against rulers, authorities, forces of cosmic darkness, and spiritual powers of evil in the heavens. Therefore, pick up the full armor of God so that you can stand your ground on the evil day and after you have done everything possible to still stand. (Ephesians 6:11-13)

Few if any figures of speech could be more familiar to the average reader or listener in Paul's day than that of the military. The Roman Empire had conquered the Mediterranean world and beyond, and a contingent stayed on to maintain the famous *Pax Romana*, the Roman peace. Thus, when Paul set out to describe a soldier's armor, his audience had the images clearly in mind. He didn't need to belabor his metaphor because the people could make applications for themselves.

Obviously, we don't have such personal knowledge. It may occur to us, however, that Paul mentions only one offensive weapon, "the sword of the Spirit, which is God's word" (6:17). The Roman soldier would also have a lance and a dagger. Perhaps Paul is suggesting that the word of God is enough, or perhaps simply like the able writer he was, he knew better than to accumulate peripheral material. The belt of truth was no doubt the leather apron a soldier wore beneath his armor or a metal belt that protected the lower abdomen. The breastplate was leather overlaid with metal, protecting the chest, and was worn only in battle.

"Put shoes on your feet," Paul said, "so that you are ready to spread the good news of peace" (6:15). Roman soldiers normally wore a half-boot, sturdy enough that they needn't worry about where they were stepping. "Above all, carry the shield of faith so that you can extinguish the flaming arrows of the evil one" (6:16). Shields were usually rectangular, made of wood and covered with leather. When armies began to use flaming arrows, their enemies quickly learned to soak their shields in water before battle to protect themselves against the "flaming arrows." The "helmet of salvation" was for the Roman soldier a helmet of brass or iron, with sidepieces to cover the cheeks. These they wore only in battle.

Several things stand out in Paul's analogy. We've noted in this description of the armor that some of the items Paul mentions were saved for times of battle. Paul makes no such distinction. Perhaps it's fair to draw the conclusion that Paul saw the Christian as always in battle. At no time can the believer lay down his or her defensive armor because the enemy of our souls never sleeps. Our Christian life is not a series of intermittent conquests or defenses but a day-by-day life of spiritual issues. I'm not suggesting that we become neurotic about temptation but only that we be wise enough to keep our helmets on and our shields ready because our enemy "is on the prowl like a roaring lion, seeking someone to devour" (1 Peter 5:8).

Note also the nature of our enemy and the nature of our battle. "We aren't fighting against human enemies," Paul reminds us, "but against rulers, authorities, forces of cosmic darkness, and spiritual powers of evil in the heavens" (Ephesians 6:12). Some pages of church history embarrass us when we recall that organized Christianity has sometimes used very unspiritual weapons, relying on physical military power in the name of Christ.

So who is our enemy? What is the nature of our battle when we gird ourselves as soldiers in conflict? In one sense Paul's language may seem very strange: "forces of cosmic darkness, and spiritual powers of evil in the heavens." Theodore O. Wedel, a leading Episcopal clergyman who was part of the generation that lived through World War II and the atrocities of extermination under Hitler and Stalin, commented, "The Enlightenment thought it had outgrown devils and demons. Our age is rediscovering their age-old power."[1]

We live some sixty years after Dr. Wedel's words, and as we read of the enslavement of tens of thousands of children being sold into sexual exploitation every year, we have to conclude that we are no more free of the demonic now than was the generation of gas chambers and willful torture; it is simply that evil has found a different venue. We ask ourselves how any human beings could participate in such brutality; "What are they thinking?" someone asks in horror. "They must be insane." And yet the SS officers of Hitler's day were often persons with doctoral degrees, and the persons participating in childhood sexual exploitation are knowledgeable enough in finance to devise ways to carry on their infamous international business.

Perhaps then we can understand Paul's language when he speaks of "cosmic darkness, and spiritual powers of evil in the heavens." When we see the human mind so corrupted, whether by its appetite for sensation or its hunger for the money that can be made by the exploitation of this appetite, we realize we're dealing with something in humanity that is irrational. In simple human speech we ask, "What gets into a person, to do such things?" The phrase is wiser than it appears; what indeed "gets into" a person?

So how do we deal with such evil? Or closer to home, with some addiction that threatens our physical, emotional, or spiritual health—addictions that others may or may not know beset us? And how do we deal with problems of self-centeredness, pettiness, and thoughtlessness, all of which are very destructive though they don't seem as demonic as the issues we've just discussed? Still, if one has engaged in such inner warfare, you know that continuing in such mental and psychological patterns is as illogical as the worst public addictions. We wonder how it is that we can recognize that such thoughts and attitudes are wrong yet continue to give them a place in our minds and lives. We know that such thoughts are unworthy of us, yet they exist and sometimes dominate. It is, for certain, a war between good and evil.

And what is our defense? What weapons do we have? The only weapon Paul mentions is the sword of the Spirit, the word of God. But it's good to remember that this is the weapon Jesus used during his intense encounter with Satan in the wilderness. Over the centuries, the greatest saints have found no better weapon than some of the great sentences from the psalms or the prophets. This same grand resource is also ours.

Then, ponder the weapons of defense that Paul recommends. We speak of the belt, the helmet, and the breastplate, but these are only the metaphorical defenses; what are the real defenses that we take into the conflict of the Christian life? Paul lists *truth, justice, peace, faith, and salvation*. These are powerful words! Truth has struggled against deception and justice against injustice for centuries and is in the fight still today. These great elements constitute the armor with which we enter the daily conflict with evil. It's the well-dressed Christian that wears such an outfit.

But Paul has another metaphor for the Christian life, very different from that of the soldier. In his letter to the people at Corinth, Paul makes a strenuous appeal for more consistent godly living. He reminds them that he has become their father in the gospel. And then this strong word: "I appeal to you, then, be imitators of me" (1 Corinthians 4:16 NRSV). Later in the same letter, he adds further strength to his metaphor: "Be imitators of me, as I am of Christ" (1 Corinthians 11:1 NRSV). He uses the same theme in writing to the Thessalonians, reminding the people that in their conversion "you became imitators of us and of the Lord" (1 Thessalonians 1:6 NRSV). But they were not limited to fashioning their lives after Paul and the Lord: "For you, brothers and sisters, became imitators of the churches of God in Christ Jesus that are in Judea" (1 Thessalonians 2:14 NRSV).

Teachers and philosophers in the first-century world often urged their students to imitate them. The emphasis was on their example as scholars. It would have been natural enough for Paul, the teacher, to have seen his converts as his students—as indeed they were—and to have had such an image in mind when he urged, "Be imitators of me."

But I envision Paul working with a more commanding and inclusive metaphor. The Greek word Paul used is the word from which we get our English word *mimic*. The essential imitator was the mimic, the actor, the person who took on not simply the intelligence or the philosophy of another person but the essence of that person as the imitator perceived him.

Theaters were common in the first-century world; after all, some of the greatest dramas date from the Greeks in 500 BC.

There were theaters not only in cities such as Athens, Antioch, Jerusalem, and Rome, but also in many smaller places. There were also traveling companies. People, no doubt, said then as we do now after a powerful performance, "I forgot that I was in a theater, watching an actor. For a while I thought it was really Willy Loman" (or Hamlet or Cleopatra).

The finest actors research their characters. They learn not only the spoken lines and the circumstances that evoked them but also how this character would respond in particular circumstances. The actor seeks, within certain artistic boundaries, to *become* that person when he is on the stage.

A good metaphor goes farther than its image. If Paul had known Shakespeare, he might have said with him, "All the world's a stage, / And all the men and women merely players. / They have their exits and their entrances."[2] And Paul would have added, "And your part is to be Christ, through all of your life, so that your fellow players will know Christ by seeing you. 'Be imitators of me, as I am of Christ.'"

This is not play-acting, and it's not a performance. Most of all, it is not an occasional event in which we seek applause. We are to try with all that is in us to be as much like our Lord as we can. And Paul gives us a head start when he urges us to imitate him, as he imitated Christ. I have made some of my best steps in the Christian life by imitating some great souls I have known. A few of these great souls were persons of recognized leadership in their area of the Christian community, but most of them were persons not known beyond their own block, so to speak, but whose beauty of character and consistency of life made me want to emulate them in my pilgrimage to imitate Christ.

This Christian life in which you and I are involved is wonderfully demanding. Anyone who thinks it is simple is only walking along the beach of its ocean, with no perception of the depths that lie even a few miles from shore. It is a life so demanding of character that one must be a very soldier to enter the daily warfare against evil, both without and within. And it is of such grandeur of living that ultimately we can describe it in only one way: I want to be like Christ.

Pictures of a Baptismal Service

by John - the heavens opened up

The story of Jesus' baptism appears in all four Gospels, and in each report, it is shown as a key factor in the beginning of his ministry. In a very real sense, it was his ordination; it was at that point that the Holy Spirit came upon Jesus, declaring him to be God's Son (Mark 1:9-11). Yet even though this baptism was so crucially significant in Jesus' life and work, he did no recorded teaching regarding baptism. Paul's baptism, on the other hand, is reported almost incidentally—that is, as an incident in the midst of several others. Yet it was Paul who left us with some key teachings about baptism. And especially, he gave us a vivid picture of baptism in a metaphor that, if we wanted, we could extend into a parable.

Perhaps it's not surprising that the reference to Paul's baptism is matter-of-fact. When a conversion is as spectacular as his, all else that happens is put in the shade. Paul (or Saul, as we know him in Acts 9) is "spewing out murderous threats" as he heads to Damascus when "suddenly a light from heaven encircled him." Its power was so great that Paul "fell to the ground." Then there was a voice, which was heard by those who were traveling with him as well as by Paul. Paul had fallen to the ground with such force that those accompanying him picked him up and found that he was blinded by the light that had overpowered him.

Paul went into Damascus as directed. He learned in a vision that a man named Ananias would pray for him and restore his sight; meanwhile, the Lord instructed Ananias to go to a house on Straight Street where he would find this notorious persecutor of Jesus' followers. Ananias proceeded in good faith, but also with some fear, to the Straight Street address. There he greeted this once-frightening but now suppliant man as "Brother Saul" and explained that Jesus had sent him so that Saul could "see again and be filled with the Holy Spirit." Then, the writer of Acts tells us, "Instantly, flakes fell from Saul's eyes and he could see again. He got up and was baptized. After eating, he regained his strength" (Acts 9:1-19).

As I said, it was all quite matter-of-fact: "He got up and was baptized," and then he ate so he could get back his strength; after all, he had been fasting for three days. This is not to suggest that baptism was incidental, but rather that it was so much a part of things that neither was it an extraordinary event. After all, in his parting words before his ascension Jesus had said, "Therefore, go and make disciples of all nations, baptizing them in the name of the Father and of the Son and of the Holy Spirit" (Matthew 28:19). So it was that on the Day of Pentecost, when the church came to birth, "Those who accepted Peter's message were baptized. God brought about three thousand people into the community on that day" (Acts 2:41).

Conversion and baptism seem to go hand in hand in the Book of Acts. For instance, at Philippi, after Paul and Silas "spoke the Lord's word" to the jailer "and everyone else in his house"—that is, his family and servants and probably the jail employees—"in the middle of the night, the jailer welcomed them and washed their wounds"; and right then, all in the household "were immediately baptized" (Acts 16:32-33). I should note in passing that two things stand out in that account, which seems like a typical one. For one, baptism was a normal, predictable part of the Christian experience; when people embraced the faith they declared their position by being baptized. Further, it was likely to be a family affair. We know nothing about the ages of the persons in the jailer's extended household; almost surely the range included children. Whatever, accepting Christianity was a family matter. One was not saved by a parent's conversion, but one came along with the head of the household.

But although Paul was himself baptized, and though he baptized at least some of his converts, apparently he did not emphasize baptism in his ministry. The church at Corinth had its favorite preachers, including Cephas (Peter), Apollos, and Paul. Paul decried this popularity culture: "Has Christ been divided? Was Paul crucified for you, or were you baptized in Paul's name?" Paul then continues, "Thank God that I didn't baptize any of you, except Crispus and Gaius, so that nobody can say that you were baptized in my name! Oh, I baptized the house of Stephanas too. Otherwise, I don't know if I baptized anyone else. Christ didn't send me to baptize but to preach the good news" (1 Corinthians 1:13-17). It appears that Paul left the baptizing to other members of his team. Perhaps this was something of his pattern of division of responsibility: he preached and gave general leadership, and others in his company baptized and perhaps saw to some of the general administrative and pastoral details.

But Paul *taught* baptism, referring to it specifically in four of his letters. He did so as he did most of the teaching in his letters, while dealing with specific questions and problems in the church. Paul was Christianity's first written theologian, but he was hardly what one would call a systematic theologian. One might say that he was a problematic theologian, in that he organized (if one can call it that) his theology around the problems the churches sent his way. Sometimes, in that process, Paul talked about secondary matters that seemed to arise naturally in discussing other matters.

And being Paul, he delivered his theology in pictures; that is, in his lively metaphors. He used several, though one stands out—partly because of its vivid quality and also because he developed it more fully.

Let's look first at some of the less-developed metaphors. In First Corinthians, Paul explains that the church is related to ancient Israel—"our ancestors," Paul calls them (1 Corinthians 10:1). Israel, he writes, "were all under the cloud and they all went through the sea. All were baptized into Moses in the cloud and in the sea" (10:1-2). The first Christians and their teachers constantly related their experiences and their theology to Israel and thus to the Hebrew Scriptures. It's unfortunate that we twenty-first-century believers don't have the same sense of family; our faith would be much richer and deeper if we did.

In this instance, Paul transposes the Christian experience of baptism onto Israel. When Israel left Egypt, a cloud led them by day and a pillar of fire by night, and at a crucial time they passed through the Red Sea. Paul explains, "See, they were just like us": they "were baptized into Moses in the cloud and in the sea." The figure of speech is stretched a bit, because the cloud that guided them did not immerse Israel, nor did the Red Sea since they passed through on dry land. But Paul wanted especially for the new believers to see that their spiritual ancestors, Israel, were baptized into Moses just as they themselves were now being baptized into Christ. In this way, Paul was also showing the relationship of the Law in the Old Testament to the grace in Christ, which was at work in the believers.

The task facing the first teachers and leaders in the church is almost beyond imagining. The basic education of the people ranged from the illiterate to the scholar. Some of the slaves who served as tutors in their master's household were no doubt in the latter category. The religious backgrounds of the believers were probably even more diverse. Some were Jews, with a knowledge of the Law and the Prophets. Others had come from cults that were more superstition than reason and still others from Greek programs that were not so much religion as ethical culture. Paul and the other apostles, prophets, evangelists, pastors, and teachers had to find ways to lead their disparate groups and individuals into consistent Christian living—which depended heavily on substantial Christian knowledge. For Paul, the metaphor was a powerful medium, as long as he could find pictures that caught the fancy of his hearers and readers.

As we've already seen and will continue to see, this sometimes meant that Paul mixed his metaphors. The mixing might come in the same paragraph or even the same sentence. Consider what Paul says to the people of Galatia. They were a difficult lot because false teachers had gone to work among them, insisting that the work of Christ was not by itself enough; they must also obey the Law of Moses, beginning with circumcision. Paul assures the Galatian believers that they "are all God's children through faith in Christ Jesus" (Galatians 3:26); then he reminds them of their baptism: "All of you who were baptized into Christ have clothed yourselves with Christ" (3:27).

How can the Galatians understand the wonder of being "baptized into Christ"? What exactly does this mean? They remember the event, which more likely than not was an experience of immersion. No doubt they also remembered the decision that preceded it and perhaps also the wonder of the emotional and spiritual experience of their conversion. But what happened when they were baptized? Paul gives them a picture: in that event they "*clothed* . . . with Christ."

It is quite possible that some of Paul's converts had previously belonged to one of the mystery cults that initiated their members by putting on a robe that symbolized a deity, suggesting that now they possessed the character and power of that god. For such persons, Paul's figure of speech was especially evocative: not only had the waters of baptism washed away the former religion and its power but also it had provided them with a new garment. There was none like it. They were now clothed with Christ. I remember a spiritual I heard in my youth: "I'm going to tell you the best thing that I ever do: I took off the old robe, and put on the new." That spiritual would have fit the Galatian baptismal experience as Paul portrayed it.

It should fit ours, as well. Baptism is surely meant to be more than a ritual, even if a time-honored one. It is more, too, than joining an organization; more even than accepting a new standard of conduct and loyalty. To be "baptized into Christ" is to clothe ourselves in him and thus to take on his very character. Obviously the ritual itself will not do this; if we give any ritual such power, we turn the ritual into cheap magic. But when the ritual is accompanied by faith, it becomes an agent for grace and reality.

The verse that follows demonstrates dramatically the new life into which we enter in Christ. William Barclay reminds us that as a practicing Jewish man Paul would have thanked God each day, "Thou hast not made me a Gentile, a slave, or a woman." But as one clothed with Christ, "There is neither Jew nor Greek; there is neither slave nor free; nor is there male and female, for you are all one in Christ Jesus" (3:28).[1] We are a new creation in Christ; our baptism is a testimony to this. When we are clothed in Christ, we lay aside the prejudices that come with society, sex, economics, race, politics, education. We see both ourselves and others primarily as we are in Christ. We are clothed in him, and we see others as similarly garbed.

Perhaps Paul's most striking picture of baptism is the one he gives us in both Romans and Colossians. It is a death, burial, and resurrection picture. This would be powerful enough in its own right, but it takes on far greater significance when placed alongside the death, burial, and resurrection of our Lord.

"Don't you know that all who were baptized into Christ Jesus were baptized into his death? Therefore, we were buried together with him through baptism into his death, so that just as Christ was raised from the dead through the glory of the Father, we too can walk in newness of life" (Romans 6:3-4). To the people at Colossae, Paul writes, "You were buried with [Christ] through baptism and raised with him through faith in the power of God, who raised him from the dead" (Colossians 2:12).

The issue is sin. Paul reminds the Colossians that they were dead because of the things they had done wrong. This put us under a debt with "requirements that worked against us." But Christ canceled all of this "by nailing it to the cross" (Colossians

2:13-14). Paul makes the same point to the Romans: "You also should consider yourselves dead to sin but alive for God in Christ Jesus" (Romans 6:11).

It's difficult for our culture really to hear what Paul is saying because we don't have Paul's understanding of sin. As we noted in an earlier chapter, Paul sees sin as a corpse that we carry about. Sin is more than a temporary lapse of character; it is the evil that subtly dogs our trail so that in a moment of inattention we do the thing we know we shouldn't do, we speak the word we know shouldn't pass our lips, and we harbor the thought that we would never want revealed to even our closest friend. Sin is not just murder, it is also the despising with which at times we look at another person; it is not only adultery but also the desire we enjoy toying with in our minds. We will not lie about some given person, but neither will we rise to their defense when we hear the lie being told about him. Sin pursues us even in our apparent righteousness: we do a good or thoughtful thing, not out of love for the other person or for God, but because we hope that others will notice our goodness and be properly impressed.

And all of this, Paul would have us know, is the way of death. To live in sin is to live deadly.

This, in turn, is why Christ died. The ultimate power of sin could be defeated only by a sinless one. So it is that Christ "died to sin once and for all with his death, but he lives for God with his life" (Romans 6:10). In the language of Charles Wesley,

> He breaks the power of canceled sin,
> he sets the prisoner free;
> his blood can make the foulest clean;
> his blood avails for me.[2]

85

Follow Paul's scenario. We humans are hopelessly afflicted with sin, the worst of it being that we don't realize how deadly our affliction is. The remedy is that a sinless one should take our infection. Christ does just this. So he dies and is buried. But because he is without sin, on the third day God raises him again. There is a resurrection. Indeed, *the* resurrection because there is no other like it.

Now then, Paul tells us, this is what it means when you are baptized. You accept Christ's death as your own, and in doing so, you reject the power of sin that crucified him. You are buried with him, and you are raised with him, into eternal life.

See, then, what happens in a baptismal service. Let's imagine the candidate is a young person or an adult; we'll call her Sarah. "Sarah has just died; died to sin. So we will bury her, as Christ was buried for her sins" (submerging the body into water, or sprinkling water on her head), "and now (raising up her body, or putting a hand firmly on her head), she is being resurrected with Christ, to live a new life by his resurrection power." If the candidate is an infant, we rejoice that a new physical life has been born into the world, then acknowledge that this child, Sarah, will in due time show that she has the universal human problem, sin, and that this is a deadly problem. By God's grace we now baptize her into Christ, in recognition that our Lord died for her salvation; and we now bury her with him and rejoice as we lift her up in his resurrection, which is also hers.

Does this death, burial, and resurrection seem unrealistic? In truth, you and I don't always look as if we are dead to sin, nor do we always look like resurrected people. But we are just that, even now: we are resurrected people, alive to Christ and alive to godly living.

If we would take hold of this truth more often, this truth would more surely take hold of us. This is what Paul knew when he told us that baptism is our death, our burial, and our eternal resurrection. He gave us the truth, and the truth is a challenge to be accepted and lived in its fullness.

Lessons in Living with Defeat

Paul was a man of grand dreams. He paid for those dreams, time and again, in having to pick up the broken pieces. We have no business reaching for the stars unless we're willing to claw our way up from the mud after stumbling in our reaching. Paul set his heart on personal achievement and found himself still reaching as he neared the end of his journey. He wanted his churches to be perfect, but Corinth was plagued by divisions, Galatia by false doctrines, and Thessalonica by apocalyptic confusion. Nevertheless, he kept on dreaming. And he believed in people, which is a place where one's heart can easily be broken, especially when you anticipate that they will become saints. "Demas has fallen in love with the present world and has deserted me" (2 Timothy 4:10); "Alexander, the craftsman who works with metal, has really hurt me" (4:14). If you believe in people, you'd better be ready for some disappointments. So, too, if people believe in you, it would be good to warn them that you may let them down.

To hope is to hurt. Those who see grand things sometimes conclude that they've suffered from faulty vision. Indeed, those who trust in God most fully are sometimes those who walk through the darkest places of God's apparent absence. Paul knew this as well as anyone and better than most. Fortunately for us, he was absolutely transparent in his letters, so we know what he went through and how he survived. He never protected his reputation by hiding his struggles and failures; he dared repeatedly to reveal his pain and his heartbreak. In the process, he left us with a metaphor that has found its place in one form or another in our common speech.

The people who give high-school commencement addresses or who speak for sales conferences and professional conventions exhort us to focus on victory. Sometimes they give the impression that there's no such thing as defeat. They have a point, of course, because if we concentrate on victory we can do a great deal to redeem our defeats and disappointments. But let's face it. Defeats are part of the fabric of life. The only way to avoid defeat is never to go into battle. I think of an amateur softball team of my youth. The manager said, "Last year we won our only game, so we decided not to play this year, so we could keep our perfect record." He had it right. The only way to be sure you never lose is never to play another game.

But the greatest souls are those persons who aim high, who stretch themselves—and thus, who take a chance on the bitterest disappointments. Paul was in that category, and I suspect that his parents encouraged him in that mindset. I think that's why they named him after a king, Saul, and provided him with a premier teacher, Gamaliel. And that's why Paul himself wanted to be the best of the spiritual achievers within his nation; that is, he wanted to be a Pharisee.

This basic compulsion didn't change when he became a Christian; it simply changed his object of dedication. As a Christian, he no longer wanted to be the best scholar or the most learned rabbi or the most meticulous Pharisee; now he wanted to be an all-out follower of Jesus Christ. He wanted to be an apostle. Others said that this couldn't possibly be because he hadn't been one of the original followers of Jesus. Indeed, Paul had never met Jesus, let alone declared his loyalty to him or walked with him day after day, for years, the way Peter, James, John, Andrew, and others did. But this didn't stop Paul. He insisted that he was as much an apostle as any of those people. And what's more, his ministry proved it. Paul worked harder than anyone else, suffered more, and was persecuted more. He started churches and won converts. Miracles followed his ministry. And of course there were his letters, which the churches passed from one to another and which constitute the achievement for which he is best known today. So judge Paul however you will—by his scholarship, by his converts, by the miracles that came through his ministry, or by the churches he established—and you have to confess that he was a winner, an achiever, a Type-A personality with some flourishes all his own.

And then, he suffered defeat. It wasn't a one-time event, like the batter who strikes out in the final game of the World Series with the bases loaded or the football player who drops the winning pass just as time runs out. Paul's defeat was a day-by-day defeat, perhaps even an hour-by-hour one. It was a defeat he carried with him, in his own body and thus also in his own psyche. He needed no enemy to remind him of it, nor some plaguing inner regret; his defeat was part of his very person, day after day.

No one knows for sure what it was. Paul names his defeat with a metaphor. He called it "a thorn in my body" or "a thorn in the flesh" (2 Corinthians 12:7 NRSV). The British scholar William Barclay said that the most accurate translation might be a *stake* in the flesh. In the first-century world, criminals sometimes were impaled on a sharp stake, and Paul said that it was this kind of stake that was twisting in his body.[1]

But what was it? What was this sharp stake, this "thorn in the flesh" that defeated Paul the rest of his life? He said, further, that it was "a messenger from Satan sent to torment" him (12:7), and that he "pleaded with the Lord three times for it to leave [him] alone" (12:8). But God said no. We'll come back to that later. At this point, I want us simply to realize that this defeat, this thorn in the flesh, was something Paul lived with until his death. And from all we can judge, it was with him every day.

So back to our question: what was this thorn in the flesh? Bible scholars have offered answers for as far back as we have any record. Some say that it was spiritual temptation or the opposition he constantly dealt with from both friends and foes. Certainly these were problems in Paul's life, but it seems to me that they are not a thorn in the *flesh* because that word speaks clearly of physical suffering rather than mental or social or psychological torment.

As for physical suffering, there are many possibilities. Malarial fever was a constant threat in that time and place. Some feel that his illness was epilepsy. Some of the earliest scholars, such as Tertullian and Jerome, felt that Paul suffered from devastating headaches, perhaps what today we know as migraine headaches. From Paul's own references, the most likely possibility would seem to be eye problems. As Paul signs the Letter to the Galatians he writes, "Look at the large letters I'm making with my own handwriting!" (Galatians 6:11). Earlier in that letter, Paul reminded the people that the reason he had first preached for them was "because of an illness. Though my poor health burdened you, you didn't look down on me or reject me." A moment later he adds, "I swear that, if possible, you would have dug out your eyes and given them to me" (4:13-15). If Paul's problem was an illness of the eyes, it was apparently of a kind that not only was handicapping but also intensely painful, and probably disfiguring in appearance, perhaps because the pain distorted the face.

If this be the case, it was a pain of several dimensions. First, physical suffering itself—itching and aching, and perhaps contributing to headaches. With it, frustration in his work: here is a scholar who cherishes his hours in the sacred and philosophical scrolls but who struggles to make out anything but the most familiar words. And if the pain causes him to contract his face and thus distract his listeners from what he is saying—well, then, we understand why he writes to the Corinthians, "I'm shy when I'm with you," and tells them he has heard that some say his letters are powerful but that in person he is weak (2 Corinthians 10:1, 10).

Whatever the thorn in the flesh, consider also its spiritual dimensions. Paul was a person whose faith often brought healing to others. As the Book of Acts reports, "God was doing unusual miracles through Paul. Even the small towels and aprons that had touched his skin were taken to the sick, and their diseases were cured and the evil spirits left them" (Acts 19:11-12). Yet he is helpless in dealing with his own illness. His critics easily could say, "Healer, heal yourself!" Each time Paul prayed for the sick and they were healed, his own illness could rise up to mock him.

I repeat, Paul never tells us what his thorn, his stake in the flesh, is. Probably he felt it was unnecessary; everyone who knew him or had ever heard of him knew what it was. Perhaps he hated to speak its name. I think still of a young farm wife in my first parish who was dying while a cancer grew steadily larger within her; in talking with me one harsh winter day she said, "This...*thing*...that is growing inside me." One hates to honor an ugliness by christening it. Perhaps it's better that we don't know what Paul's illness was because, if we did, it probably would be known still today by that name: "Paul's Thorn."

Instead Paul gave us a metaphor. As a result, any of us can claim it for our own when we deal with, and perhaps live with, some pain of body or anguish of mind and soul that seems to hold us captive. We have "a thorn in the flesh," we say; a stake driven into the very soul.

I am profoundly grateful that I don't have to conclude our lesson here. If you have such a thorn—whether of body, mind, psyche, or spirit—I urge you first of all not to give up. Paul dared to ask God three times for God to remove his thorn. I calculate that in mercy for a weaker soul like me, God might permit me to ask still longer.

Also, God told Paul directly that he would not get the healing he desired; specifically, he was better off with the illness than with the healing. If you or I struggle with some thorn, we might well ask God to grant us the same favor. I'm suggesting, that is, that we may rightly keep asking for our thorn—whether in the flesh, the mind, the temperament, the memory—to be removed unless God makes clear that it is better that we keep it. I'm sure we sometimes acquiesce to a thorn, not out of a sense of God's purposes but from human weariness. We endure when we should persevere.

God's answer to Paul was very specific. "'My grace is enough for you, because power is made perfect in weakness.' So I'll gladly spend my time," Paul said, "bragging about my weaknesses so that Christ's power can rest on me. Therefore, I'm all right with weaknesses, insults, disasters, harassments, and stressful situations for the sake of Christ, because when I'm weak, then I'm strong" (2 Corinthians 12:9-10).

Paul wants us to know that he is a better person with the thorn than without it. Did his own sickness diminish his ability to be an instrument of healing to others? No; to the contrary, he now could do far better. Long ago I knew a young man who looked like a model for a Charles Atlas advertisement. His muscles all but rippled. He confessed with real sorrow that he found it hard to empathize with those who were ill; physical weakness was outside the realm of his experience and even of his imagination. A thorn in the flesh might have given my friend a quality of compassion that would have driven him to more effectual prayer for sufferers and more empathetic listening. Mind you, however, this is not guaranteed. Some people with a thorn in the flesh simply become more self-centered, so that when a battered soul begins telling of their pain, this person answers, "You think *you've* got troubles? I'm an *authority* on trouble! You think you've got a *thorn*? There's no problem in translation for me: what I have is a *stake,* and it revels in my pain night and day." We can cheapen our thorn into a justification for self-pity.

A thorn in the spirit is more subtle and more complicated and often, therefore, more difficult to recognize. Here is a man or a woman or a teenager whose thorn in the spirit is sexual temptation. This person doesn't act physically on the temptation, but when the thought enters his mind, he metaphorically clears off a chair and invites the thought to settle in for a while.

The thorn has no immediate sting; to the contrary, it's rather pleasing. Then there's the person to whom this individual dares one day to confess his struggle. Unfortunately, the person with whom he shares is a person whose thorn in the spirit is self-righteousness. This person happens to know little about sexual temptation. He listens with careful detachment and says confidently, "You'll have to get over that. To begin with, you ought to be ashamed of yourself." Self-righteousness is so dangerous because we don't know it's a thorn; self-righteousness is an illness that grows within and doesn't assert itself until it demands major surgery. You can live with it for years and rarely feel even a modest discomfort. "When I finally came to see what I was like," a truly fine soul said to me, "it made me sick to my stomach. How in God's name could I have dared to pass judgment on anyone else?"

Some of the greatest souls have suffered with a thorn in the spirit: one thinks of Saint John of the Cross and of Mother Teresa, both of whom wrestled with the dark night of the soul, the feeling of God's distance, even of God's absence. Such persons are driven to hold on to God when God seems disinterested in their clinging. They hold all the more fiercely because they believe in the character of God intellectually and by faith, even though emotionally there is no reassuring voice.

I think Paul would have said that he preferred a thorn in the flesh. I know this would be my choice, if a choice were given. I would cry with David of old, "Please don't throw me out of your presence; / please don't take your holy spirit away from me" (Psalm 51:11). Paul received God's assurance that he was a better person and a more fruitful believer with his thorn in the flesh than without it. If he had gotten rid of the thorn in the flesh, it would have been at the cost of something vital in his spirit.

Perhaps it would have meant an arrogance; I suspect this came easily for Paul, and with reason, because he really was brighter and more steadfast than most of us. Or perhaps he would have lost some of the transparency that makes him and his writing so priceless and so encouraging. He surely would have lost some of the depth of understanding that comes only with defeat.

The athlete's sweatshirt says, "There's Nothing Like Winning." But Paul and the saints (and many a wise person who might never claim saintliness) would say that there is, however, something *better* than winning, and that is defeat from which one has learned. When we see the value in defeat, it is no longer a defeat. It is nothing other than a step to victory. A step toward greater, more substantial, more utterly true victory.

I have lived long enough to have accumulated a substantial quota of defeats. I was a pastor long enough to become a statistician in knowing the defeats of other persons. I'm enough of a lover of history and biography to know how large a part defeat has played in the shaping of our world. Above all, I have lived in the Bible, the ultimate textbook in the exquisite agony and the majestic value of defeat. There is a cross, and there is a resurrection, and there cannot be a resurrection without a cross.

Paul had a word for it: a *thorn*, a *stake*. He had a specific locale: in the flesh. Whatever your thorn and whatever its locale, listen to Paul. Pray for the thorn's removal, and be grateful if it is taken from you. But if God says no, listen: there is grace for you (amazing grace!), and God's power is made perfect at our place of weakness.

The Christian Life
Beyond Words

Of all the gifts God has entrusted to us human beings, nothing compares with the gift of words. Whether spoken or written, they make us what we are. Far more than the opposable thumb or the ability to walk upright, words make us human. We glory in the human ability to reason, but this reasoning has its primary form of structure and communication via words. We wax sentimental about our capacity for feelings, but most of the time those feelings search for words as a means of conveyance. True, there are times when we abandon words in expressing our feelings and turn instead to a touch, an embrace, or a kiss, and indeed at times a word almost seems to intrude on a feeling; but before long, we return to the necessity of words.

And yet, powerful as words are, and extensive as the human vocabulary grows, there are times and experiences that go beyond words. "I wish I could find the words," we say helplessly, thinking that somewhere out there in the realm of language there must be a way to say what we have experienced.

Our experiences themselves are the problem: we can experience things that leave us without words. Sometimes it's "the funniest thing you ever heard," but when we report it to our friends, we sense that something is missing and we add, apologetically, "I guess you'd have to have been there." So too with some of life's most heartwarming experiences. Even before we begin to report such experiences, we know that the other person can't grasp what has happened to us because we don't have vocabulary adequate to express it.

This is especially true in the realm of religious experience. Even Paul, the master theologian, the greatest of letter writers, a person skilled in several languages, came to a place beyond words. Then he did what we often do at such a time. He found a metaphor. As it happens, it was an old metaphor. But let this be a lesson to us all. Sometimes it's much better to use an old metaphor that works than to scramble for a new one that falls flat.

As we have noted earlier, there were those in the early church who questioned Paul's authority. This was primarily because he hadn't seen Jesus in the flesh. Thousands of people could testify that they had heard Jesus teach, had seen him perform miracles, or had been part of a multitude that he had fed. Paul had no such experience. He was a latecomer, as he himself confessed. John could write that he was telling about "what we have seen with our eyes, what we have seen and our hands handled" (1 John 1:1), but Paul couldn't make such a statement. Then one day he had an experience that was as real as anything anyone might have known in the days of Jesus' ministry on earth.

Paul tells this story in the third person. "I know a man in Christ who was caught up into the third heaven fourteen years ago" (2 Corinthians 12:2). "I'll brag about this man," Paul tells us, "but I won't brag about myself, except to brag about my weaknesses" (12:5). We know Paul is talking about himself. His people in Corinth knew so, as well. Paul knew that they would. But he wanted his readers to know how inappropriate it would be to tell this experience in the first person singular. He knew he was unworthy of what had happened to him. It's clear at many times in Paul's letters that he struggled with his ego as much as many of us do and probably more than some. He was by nature a strong, ambitious man. But he was holy enough and perceptive enough to recognize his problem, and he intended to do everything in his power to protect himself from the kind of egotism that would corrupt his soul and weaken his witness.

Whatever experience Paul is recalling, it was in a class by itself. Paul was a tough-minded scholar, but he had also had more than his share of what most of us would see as mystical experiences. The Book of Acts reports several occasions where Paul had visions and where he experienced divine interventions in his work. We sometimes assume that a scholarly, philosophical type of person has no room for religious experience. There is evidence enough to the contrary. One thinks especially of Blaise Pascal (1623–1662), one of history's true geniuses. He was a mathematician, a scientist, a philosopher, and a literary artist, but he was also a person of deep Christian faith who knew God at an experiential level. One night he encountered God in an event of such reality that he wrote it down and then sewed the document into the lining of his jacket; a servant found it there after his death. Pascal prefaced the record of that memorable night by noting the exact time it happened: "In the year of Grace, 1654, On Monday, 23rd of November, Feast of St. Clement, Pope and Martyr, and of others in the Martyrology, Vigil of Saint Chrysogonus, martyr and others, From about half past ten in the evening until about half past twelve." And then, as if to title what follows, Pascal wrote, "FIRE."[1] Paul was not a scientist or a mathematician in the manner of Blaise Pascal, but he was a true scholar, the kind of person who would put his experiences to test so that he could be sure they were more than a hallucination or an emotion of the moment.

And let me note again that religious experiences were not new to Paul. For instance, when he and his team planned to travel through Phrygia and Galatia, "the Holy Spirit kept them from" doing so when they approached the province of Mysia (Acts 16:6-7). The writer doesn't tell us how the Spirit interfered, but he does tell us what happened next: "A vision of a man from Macedonia came to Paul during the night. He stood urging Paul, 'Come over to Macedonia and help us!'" (16:9). It was after this vision when Paul took the path that led into his ministry in what we now call Europe.

Paul had another such nighttime visitation when he was in Corinth: "One night the Lord said to Paul in a vision, 'Don't be afraid. Continue speaking. Don't be silent. I'm with you and no one who attacks you will harm you, for I have many people in this city'" (18:9-10). Some years later when Paul was in Jerusalem, praying in the Temple, he had another "visionary experience." This time God was instructing Paul to "leave Jerusalem at once," because he would be rejected there (22:17-18). Still later, on a perilous sea trip to Rome, Paul went public with a vision, when he urged the men on his ship to break their fast because the previous night "an angel from the God to whom I belong and whom I worship stood beside me" and assured Paul that he would safely reach his destination (27:21-26).

I refer to these experiences to make clear that Paul was no stranger to the world of the supernatural. I see nothing in his writings or in the record in Acts to suggest that Paul sought such experiences. It seems, rather, that such experiences were a customary part of his spiritual life. I sense that they were a necessary factor in his extraordinary missionary travels. I see Paul as a highly organized person, someone who planned ahead in the confidence that he was doing God's business and that God would correct him if he were on the wrong track. And as the record reports it, such was sometimes the case. The world of spiritual experience was a component of daily life to those pioneers of the gospel. But none of those experiences could compare with what happened on that special day that was beyond words. This experience was of such a quality that Paul couldn't help boasting about it. He confessed that boasting was inappropriate; thus he shelters his statement by telling his story in the third person. If he were going to boast, Paul tells us, he would boast about the man who had such an experience as this.

Nevertheless, important as this experience was, Paul doesn't really tell his readers what happened. It was a "You had to have been there" sort of report. He gives us only one physical detail: it happened "fourteen years ago." He doesn't give us the kind of precise dating that Pascal offers, but he wants us to know that the time is set forever in his mind. One scholar calculates that this would have been circa AD 44. Nor does Paul identify the place where it happened. As far as he's concerned the physical location was incidental because "I don't know whether it was in the body or out of the body. God knows" (2 Corinthians 12:2).

This much, however, Paul does know: whether it was in the body or in the spirit, this man "was caught up into the third heaven" (12:2). In the following verse Paul describes this "third heaven" as "paradise," and there, he tells us, "he heard unspeakable words that were things no one is allowed to repeat." Again he tells us that he doesn't know whether this man was "in the body or apart from the body. God knows."

I admit that I am uneasy when someone tells me that "God told them" something. I don't doubt their sincerity or their personal integrity; it's just that I am very conscious of our human capacity for error. I'm impressed that Paul was careful never to put words in God's mouth. Thus when laying out some moral standards to the people in Corinth, he carefully modifies his statements, as to whether he is giving his own opinion or is speaking by command from God. "I don't have a command from the Lord about people who have never been married, but I'll give you my opinion as someone you can trust because of the Lord's mercy" (1 Corinthians 7:25). It is this very cautious language that gives substance to the divine inspiration with which Paul writes.

We will never know what Paul heard in his ecstatic experience. We know only that the words were "unspeakable"; "things no one is allowed to repeat." That's a tantalizing description! We can only conclude that Paul sensed that what he was hearing and seeing was for his edification alone. Perhaps God was reassuring him that he was forgiven for the pain he brought to so many during the period when he was persecuting the early believers. We know that this memory haunted him. He defended his right to be recognized as an apostle, but still, he said, "I don't deserve to be called an apostle, because I harassed God's church" (1 Corinthians 15:9).

Or perhaps this was Paul's equivalent to the sacred encounter Moses experienced when God set him "in a gap in the rock" and covered him there until a holy moment when Moses could see God's back (Exodus 33:21-23). There's something theologically appealing in this approach—that God entrusted Moses to deliver the Law, then gave Paul the assignment to deliver the message of grace, and that God favored both men with unique divine encounters. But in saying this I'm only speculating with you, simply to give us some sense of what might have been going on in Paul's pilgrimage, and why it was that God chose to give him such an extraordinary experience—an experience that Paul could describe only as being in "the third heaven."

Let me dare one further speculation. When Paul gives his magnificent exposition on Christ's resurrection, he lists a number of persons or groups that witnessed the resurrected Christ, then adds himself, "last of all," one who came into the faith late, but nevertheless, Christ "appeared also to me" (1 Corinthians 15:8 ESV). Was Paul referring to this experience, this sacred time when he didn't know if he himself was in or out of the body; was this his hour of seeing the resurrected Christ? Was this what Paul meant when he declared that the resurrected Christ "appeared also to me"? Peter, James, and John had a kind of pre-Resurrection experience on the Mount of Transfiguration (Matthew 17:1-8); was Paul's experience "in the body or out of the body" his post-Resurrection experience?

Whatever happened, Paul said it was beyond words. And whatever was said to him, he knew he dared not repeat it. The best Paul could say, he said in his metaphor: it was an experience in "the third heaven." As I said earlier, the metaphor was not original with Paul. Come to think of it, originality is not the test of a metaphor; the only test is that the metaphor helps convey a meaning that we would not otherwise be able to express or to grasp.

Ancient Jewish writings, which were no doubt part of Paul's knowledge, had various ideas of the number of heavens. Three and seven were the numbers mentioned most often, probably because these numbers had a mystical quality of their own. In any event, the phrase "the third heaven" carried the idea of the farthest spiritual reach.

Our contemporary culture doesn't speak of heaven as freely as our grandparents did, nor do we sing about it as much—and that's a pity. It's not surprising therefore that our secular culture has produced a secular substitute: we say that something altogether out of the ordinary is "out of this world." Our contemporary culture isn't sure enough of heaven to say that something is heavenly, but we do the best we can with our secular limitations—"out of this world." Perhaps it's just as well that we limit our secular experiences to secular metaphors.

But Paul had experienced something that was not only out of this world, it was in *another* world and an altogether real one. Was it a physical transport? Paul tells us twice that he doesn't know whether he was in the body or out of the body. The important fact was a spiritual one: he had known a nearness to God beyond description and beyond anything he could hope for in his earthly lifetime. Fourteen years had elapsed since the experience, and clearly he never again had known anything to compare with it. Of course not. It was an experience in heavenly places, one he did not expect to duplicate short of eternity itself.

Whatever "the third heaven" may be, is Paul's experience something you or I might have? In case you're wondering (and you probably aren't), I've never had such an experience. I've been blessed with great and memorable times; more than my share, I'm sure. Some have come during the singing of beloved hymns and others at an electric moment during a sermon. Still others have come during conversations with a fellow believer when there was no doubt but that Christ was also present. And quiet times, when God has let me see my own heart and, after that, his love. There's an expression among the devout in the Scottish highlands: the air there, they say, is "very thin." The sense of God's presence is peculiarly real and immediate. I cherish the hours of my annual pilgrimage to the world of my growing up and of my young manhood, where memory reminds me of the saints I have known and of the experiences that have shaped my life. But would I say that I was in a "third heaven"? No. They've been lovely, and experiences for which I am profoundly thankful, but not a third heaven.

Paul does leave us, however, with a significant phrase. When he begins to tell the story of his extraordinary experience, he uses a term that is key to his whole theology of spiritual reality when he describes himself this way: "I know a man *in Christ* who was caught up into the third heaven" (2 Corinthians 12:2, Italics mine). This was Paul's unceasing goal, that he would be *in Christ*. This was the goal he cherished for all his believers. There is no magic in the Christian practice that comes through the uttering of mystical words, no posture of unique power, no formula of preparation, and no ground that is guaranteed to be holy. But there is a state of mind and soul that comes into its own, over time, as we become less concerned with self and more concerned with Christ and others. Then, our residence is *in Christ*.

I don't know where the third heaven is. I don't believe there is any secret formula for getting there. But I'm altogether sure that it is possible (though perhaps only if one needs it desperately), and that it is to be found only where Paul found it—*in Christ*.

This Mortal and Immortal Flesh

The New Testament tells us next to nothing about the physical appearance of its lead characters. Most of us have some ideas of our own. These ideas are probably an amalgam of the religious paintings or movie portrayals we've seen, or what our imaginations have done with the sermons we've heard and the poems or stories we've read. The average person, including the religiously indifferent, is quite sure he or she knows what Jesus looked like though there's not a single word in the four books that tell his story—Matthew, Mark, Luke, and John—that gives even a hint of Jesus' height, weight, complexion, eye color, or facial features.

We know a little about Paul, primarily from what he himself said. But one has to be careful how much that brief comment reveals and how much we supplement it from our own prior feelings. "I know what some people are saying," Paul writes to the Corinthians: "'His letters are severe and powerful, but in person he is weak and his speech is worth nothing'"

(2 Corinthians 10:10). We might see these words as evidence of the powerful impact of Paul's letters; certainly the centuries have proved as much. After all, no letter writer in human history has influenced the world longer and in greater breadth and depth than Paul. At the same time, however, another response is clear. As persuasive as Paul was in his writing, his physical appearance was unimpressive; so much so that when he was present, people discounted his letters on the basis of his bodily person.

A document from the late second century gives us further information. It is fascinating, but perhaps it adds more to our speculation than to reliable knowledge. Scholars calculate that it reflects an oral tradition that was passed on into the second century. It describes Paul as "a man of middling size, and his hair was scanty, and his legs were a little crooked, and his knees were projecting, and he had large eyes and his eyebrows met, and his nose was somewhat long, and he was full of grace and mercy; at one time he seemed like a man, and at another time he seemed like an angel." The person describing Paul apparently wanted us to know that his physical person was not prepossessing but that his character more than made up for that lack. In this, the second-century memory seems to endorse what Paul reported in his letter, that he was not a commanding physical presence.

As we have noted earlier, Paul suffered from one or more physical ailments—problems enough and ever-present enough that he could look upon the body as sometimes a burden. Nevertheless, his use of sports metaphors makes us feel that he had great respect for the capacity of the physical body. When he describes the Christian life as a race, he gives tacit recognition to the Grecian sculpture that saw the beauty of the disciplined human body.

Paul also knew, however, that the body presents us humans with unique perils. Paul saw sin as a problem in many forms, including mind and spirit. But he was not such a detached philosopher or theologian as to forget that the body presents particular temptations. He pictured the struggle in vigorous physical terms. "I fight like a boxer in the ring, not like someone who is shadowboxing. Rather, I'm landing punches on my own body and subduing it like a slave. I do this to be sure that I myself won't be disqualified after preaching to others" (1 Corinthians 9:26-27). Paul knew that at times his body was an enemy to be subdued. Or perhaps we should say, as a part of one's person that sometimes goes in revolt against our best interests, so that we must struggle to hold in check this rebellious element of our person. No wonder then that he wanted to pummel his body the way a trained boxer beats on the body of an opponent. Such is the language with which the apostle describes the perils he faced in his own body and that he sensed troubled the people to whom he preached. The body can be a friend or an enemy. It is God's creation, beautiful in its potential, but nevertheless able to destroy the character and the soul to which it is related. Yes, Paul knew a great deal about the body. He was a human being, and he was candid enough with his believers to let them know that the body is, among other things, a force to be reckoned with.

It's all the more dangerous because it is an integral part of who we are because it is woven together with our minds, our psyches, and our spirits. Touch the body and you also touch the soul. Let the body make a decision and it makes a decision for the whole person. Paul put it in straightforward fashion when he wrote to the people at Rome, "So then, don't let sin rule your body, so that you do what it wants" (Romans 6:12). But don't think that Paul's attitude toward the body was a kind of delicate Puritanism that saw the body as a packaged explosive of evil, just waiting to destroy. He continues, "Instead, present yourselves to God as people who have been brought back to life from the dead, and offer all the parts of your body to God to be used as weapons to do right. Sin will have no power over you, because you aren't under Law but under grace" (Romans 6:13-14).

Nor does Paul think that some parts of the body are hopelessly inclined to evil, as did some of the philosophers of his day and ours; "*all* the parts of your body," he writes, can "be used as weapons to do right." He's so sure of this that he sees a time when the Lord Jesus Christ "will transform our humble bodies so that they are like his glorious body, by the power that also makes him able to subject all things to himself" (Philippians 3:21). In other words, this human body has the power, on one hand, of ultimate self-destruction, and on the other of being like the resurrected, "glorious" body of the Lord Christ.

So where did Paul find a metaphor for the body? As we've already observed, he got metaphors from the Olympics to the military and from wedding garments to a pot for the garbage. Well, when it comes to the body he turns to sacred architecture: the temple.

For Paul, it was not just any temple. He had a temple image in his mind that was as old as Sinai. "Do you not know that your body is a temple of the Holy Spirit within you, which you have from God, and that you are not your own? For you were bought with a price; therefore glorify God in your body" (1 Corinthians 6:17-20 NRSV). What, as Paul sees it, is your body, or mine? It is *the temple of God.*

I repeat, for Paul, this was the most daring of metaphors. But we have to get into Paul's mind and his experience to get the metaphor's full impact. The Jews had a profound, unique commitment to their place of worship. It began with their birth as a people. The same book, Exodus, that gave them the Law also gave them the instructions and data for their house of worship. This was not by chance. The Law provided standards for a way of life, and the temple and its worship provided the spiritual energy to live such a life and to find forgiveness and restoration when their daily living fell short.

Israel's first temple was in fact a portable tabernacle that they constructed and then carried with them on their journey from slavery to their land of promise. The plans for its building are so detailed that we're likely to find them tedious reading. But the careful spelling-out of each element in this portable building demonstrates how special the building was to be. Even though it was a temporary structure and one that could be taken down when the nation moved on, then set up again when they were in a place for whatever period of time, it was sacred in all its parts. At that point, Israel was a nomadic people, but they had a temple, a place of worship, a center for their life as a people. The tabernacle's location said as much. It was in the middle of the encampment, with three tribes on each of the four sides. Their portable house of worship was at the center of their mobile nation for some forty years.

When at last Israel got a permanent house of worship, it was ornate nearly to a fault, and every part carried sacred significance. Solomon's prayer at the Temple's dedication may well have been the high point of his reign. It was a Temple "for the name of the LORD," a place where the people could repent and return to God when they had wandered from him, and where

the immigrant would always be welcome. Yet even as he dedicated the building Solomon confessed, "If heaven, even the
highest heaven, can't contain you, how can this temple that I've
built contain you?" (1 Kings 8:27). Several centuries later, in the
nation's loneliest hour, when enemy armies destroyed Jerusalem,
the worst of it was the demolishing of their Temple. The writer
of Lamentations saw this destruction as God's judgment: "My
Lord rejected his altar, he abandoned his sanctuary; / he handed
Zion's palace walls over to enemies. / They shouted in the LORD's
own house as if it were a festival day" (Lamentations 2:7). The
ultimate indignity of Israel's defeat came in their enemy's treat-
ing Israel's Temple as it if were their own.

All of which is to say that for a devout Jew, nothing conveyed
a greater sense of sacredness than the temple, whether it was
the portable sanctuary they carried through the wilderness, or
the Temple Solomon built or even the ruins that remained after
an enemy invasion. So now Paul, with his poignant sense of
the specialness of this place, makes the temple his metaphor for
the human body. *Any* human body, if its occupant has chosen
to become a follower of Christ. The body of a believer carried
this profound sacredness, not only if the bearer was an apostle
or a teacher, but just as surely for woman or man, slave or free,
Gentile or Jew. The bodies of those who know Christ are the
temple of God.

Paul's metaphor had a logical base. The new people of God,
Christians, were the people of the Holy Spirit. When the Spirit
came on the Day of Pentecost, those who were there "were all
filled with the Holy Spirit" (Acts 2:4, italics mine). There were
evidences in wind, fire, and tongues, but the event itself was an
infilling of the Spirit of God. This occasion is sometimes referred
to as a baptism in the Spirit, which is an impressive term in its

own right, but its language is comparatively limited. When the Holy Spirit comes to the believer, it is not only like a physical immersion but also much more; it is a filling and an indwelling of the Holy Spirit. The believer is someone in whom the Spirit of God dwells. That is, the believer is now a *temple* of God.

It is on this ground that Paul pleads for sexual purity. Prostitution was not only common and unrestricted in many parts of the first-century world but also tied to the popular religions. If you travel to the ancient city of Corinth, your tour guide is likely to pause at what was once the city's center and point to a nearby hillside where the prostitutes of pagan religions operated. Paul knew something of such a practice from a dark time in his own nation's history. There was a time when Israel had departed so far from their faith that such practices were pursued in their own temple, so that when King Josiah instituted his great reform, "He broke down the houses of the male temple prostitutes that were in the house of the LORD" (2 Kings 23:7 NRSV). In Paul's world as in ours, sexual sin was a dominant issue. He based his appeal for sexual purity on the sacredness of the human body. "Avoid sexual immorality!" Paul commands. "Don't you know that your body is a temple of the Holy Spirit who is in you? Don't you know that you have the Holy Spirit from God, and you don't belong to yourselves? You have been bought and paid for, so honor God with your body" (1 Corinthians 6:18-20).

But with all of that, Paul recognizes that this body is *mortal*. *Mortal* is one of those words that we use without realizing the decisive content of its meaning. If you belonged to the generation or to a school system that encouraged the study of Latin, you will remember that *mortal* comes from the Latin word *mors, mortis*—which means "death." Thus, to be mortal is to be a dying creature, a creature that from the time of birth is headed to death.

Paul knew that we are mortal; death is part of our basic description. But he also knew that there is more to us than that. He assures us that a time will come "when the rotting body has been clothed in what can't decay, and the dying body has been clothed in what can't die" (1 Corinthians 15:54); or as the New Revised Standard Version puts it, a time when "this mortal body puts on immortality." There is much more to us than appears on the surface!

It's with the strength of this conviction that Paul encourages those who are suffering. He knows that some of his beloved converts are "experiencing all kinds of trouble....We are knocked down, but we aren't knocked out" (2 Corinthians 4:8-9). Now Paul turns to another metaphor. He speaks of the human body as "the tent that we live in on earth." This tent may be "torn down"; but if that happens, "we have a building from God. It's a house that isn't handmade, which is eternal and located in heaven." It's no wonder, then, if "we groan while we live in this residence. We really want to dress ourselves with our building from heaven—since we assume that when we take off this tent, we won't find out that we are naked" (2 Corinthians 5:1-3).

Don't be surprised that when Paul describes our human bodies, he comes up with such different pictures. We are the temple of God; you can't be more extraordinary than that! But we're also tents that will be disposed of someday; this suggests that our bodies are quite dispensable. Or to put it another way, these bodies are mortal because from the day we're born our bodies begin to die. But our bodies are also immortal, and that immortality will take over at the right time.

Paul knew what he was talking about. His body had taken a full share of the blows of outrageous fortune, some of them through a variety of illnesses and others through beatings and imprisonment and treacherous travel. He knew about the temptations of the body, too, partly from what he had seen in the lives of his followers and no doubt from his own bodily tests.

But he knew more; much, much more. He knew that his body was so uniquely energized that when the mortal was asserting itself, the immortal was stronger than ever. And he knew that he needn't worry too much about his physical body because it was only a tent, a temporary dwelling, while a body not made with hands awaited him. And however inadequate his physical body might seem at times, and no matter how people might find his physical person unprepossessing, his body (and ours too) was the very temple of the Holy Spirit. Solomon had said that if the heaven of heavens could not contain the Lord God, how much less any temple we might build. Paul knew that his human body—no matter what anyone might think of it—was adequate to house the Spirit of God.

Out postmodern world thinks highly of the body. Medical science is managing daily to extend our physical life expectancy. The ubiquitous health centers promise to make us all as appealing as Greek statuary, and fashion designers are finding ways to make the most of those features that the health centers can't help.

But at their absolute best and with all their combined efforts, they haven't the good news that Paul knew. We are tents that will one day be replaced with an eternity-brand label. And we are temples in which the Spirit of God is pleased to dwell.

Notes

Introduction

1. Harry Shaw, *Dictionary of Literary Terms* (New York: McGraw-Hill, 1972), 235.

2. Shaw, *Dictionary*, 274.

2. The Christian Life as a Sports Fan Sees It

1. A. C. Bouquet, *Everyday Life in New Testament Times* (New York: Charles Scribner's Sons, 1954), 41.

2. Michael Glerup, *Gregory of Nyssa, Sermons on the Beatitudes* (Downers Grove, IL: IVP Books, 2012), 40.

3. Sin and I

1. J. Budziszewski, "This Time Will Not Be the Same," *First Things* (March 2014): 24.

2. Craig S. Keener, *The IVP Bible Background Commentary, Second Edition* (Downers Grove, IL: IVP Academic, 2014), 438.

3. As quoted in Thomas G. Long, Thomas Lynch, *The Good Funeral* (Louisville: Westminster John Knox, 2013), 91.

4. Stan Key, "The Gap."

4. Vessels in the King's House

1. Eugene Peterson, *The Message* (Colorado Springs: Navpress, 1993), 321.

2. John Wesley, "A Covenant Prayer in the Wesleyan Tradition," *The United Methodist Hymnal* (Nashville: The United Methodist Publishing House, 1989), 607.

5. The Christian's Larger Family

1. Craig S. Keener, *The IVP Bible Background Commentary, Second Edition* (Downers Grove, IL: IVP Academic, 2014), 167.

2. John Knox, *The Interpreter's Bible, Volume 9* (Nashville: Abingdon Press, 1954), 517.

3. William Barclay, *The Mind of St. Paul* (New York: Harper & Row, 1958), 32.

7. Portraits of the Church

1. William Barclay, *The Mind of St. Paul* (New York: Harper & Row, 1958), 252.

8. The Christian as Soldier and as Actor

1. Theodore O. Wedel, *The Interpreter's Bible, Volume 10* (Nashville: Abingdon Press, 1953), 737.

2. William Shakespeare, *As You Like It*, act 2, scene 7, line 139.

9. Pictures of a Baptismal Service

1. William Barclay, *The Letters to the Galatians and Ephesians* (Philadelphia: Westminster, 1954, 1958), 35.

2. Charles Wesley, "O for a Thousand Tongues to Sing," *The United Methodist Hymnal* (Nashville: The United Methodist Publishing House, 1989), 57.

10. Lessons in Living with Defeat

1. William Barclay, *The Letters to the Corinthians* (Philadelphia: Westminster, 1954, 1956), 287.

11. The Christian Life Beyond Words

1. Steve Ham, In God We Trust: Why Biblical Authority Matters for Every Believer (Green Forest, AR: Master Books, 2010), 12.

Discussion Guide for J. Ellsworth Kalas's
The Parables of Paul

John D. Schroeder

CHAPTER 1
THE SLAVE: A SELF-PORTRAIT

Summary

This chapter examines why Paul calls himself a slave of Christ Jesus, why it is a title of achievement, and what it means to be a slave.

Discussion Questions

1. What does the author tell us about Paul's use of metaphors? What are the distinctions he makes between metaphors and parables?
2. How was Paul both an apostle and a prisoner? Why were these titles appropriate?
3. Why did Paul use the same metaphor in his letterhead on three occasions? What were those three occasions?
4. What does the author say about the institution of slavery in Roman times?
5. Why did Paul want to be seen and remembered as a slave?

6. What is Paul saying about both Jesus and himself in Philippians 2:6-7?
7. What does Paul say about slavery in his letter to the Romans?
8. Did Paul have a healthy self-image? What factors and experiences contributed toward his self-image?
9. Name some of the ways we act as slaves in serving others in Christ's name.
10. How do we live out this life as Christ's slave?

Prayer

Dear God, thank you for giving us the privilege of serving you in so many ways. Thank you for the example and ministry of Paul regarding how to live for you. Help us to remember you are always with us. Amen.

CHAPTER 2
THE CHRISTIAN LIFE AS A SPORTS FAN SEES IT

Summary

This chapter explores life as a Christian and why Paul used a metaphor to compare it to participating in a sport. It also reminds us that rewards are temporary and encourages us to practice self-denial and dedication, as athletes do.

Discussion Questions

1. Why do you think sports have such a wide appeal? What is a favorite sport of yours, and why this particular one?
2. Explain what made Paul qualified to be the apostle to the Gentiles.

3. What does the author tell us about the Isthmian games?
4. What points is Paul trying to get across to us in the sports metaphors about races and boxing that he uses in First Corinthians?
5. Compare and contrast the sort of crown that athletes compete to win with the crown that Christians strive to win. What are the differences?
6. What do practicing sports and practicing Christianity have in common?
7. Paul reminds us that many rewards are temporary. Why is that the case?
8. List some benefits of practicing self-denial and dedication. What are the positive contexts of doing so as it relates to the Christian life?
9. What are some of the potential dangers of spiritual shallowness?
10. How might feeling that "death is near" change a person's life, attitude, and actions?

Prayer

Dear God, thank you for being with us as we participate in all aspects in life. Save us from the dangers of spiritual shallowness and encourage us to practice self-denial and dedication as we strive to win the crown and become better Christians. Amen.

CHAPTER 3
SIN AND I

Summary

This chapter looks at sin through the eyes of Paul. It illustrates his spiritual struggles and provides advice for our own struggles.

Paul uses the metaphor of a corpse to help us understand the reality of sin in our lives.

Discussion Questions

1. When did you begin to understand sin and start taking it seriously?
2. Why do we often take sin lightly or try to ignore it?
3. Explain why as the author said, "Sin was a reality to Paul."
4. What does Paul say about his own spiritual struggles?
5. Explain the meaning behind Romans 7:24. What point was Paul making here with his metaphor about a "dead corpse"?
6. According to the author, what "double therapy" does Paul hope to achieve by his testimony?
7. Explain what the author calls "the unnerving part" of the corpse metaphor; why was the idea of carrying a corpse "especially repugnant" to the readers of Paul's letters and a sensitive subject for Paul to raise?
8. What role does the blurring of standards play in our recognition and acknowledgment of sin?
9. Why was a corpse an excellent choice as a metaphor for sin?
10. What kind of metaphor for sin might we use today?

Prayer

Dear God, thank you for reminding us of the dangers of sin. Help us to remember Paul's metaphor and his advice when we struggle spiritually. May we always remember your love and availability to help in times of trouble. Amen.

CHAPTER 4
VESSELS IN THE KING'S HOUSE

Summary

This chapter examines why Paul uses images of a potter and clay to help us understand our service to God. It reminds us that we are members of the King's household and that we serve as his vessels.

Discussion Questions

1. What is your image of the kingdom of heaven?
2. When we pray, "Thy kingdom come," what are we saying?
3. How is the kingdom of heaven different from any other kingdom?
4. Why does Paul use "the world of pottery" to make his point?
5. Using this theme from Jeremiah, what was Paul trying to tell Christians in Rome?
6. Explain why it is important to remember that any role in the King's household is a privilege.
7. Where do you perform most effectively? Name some of your own limits.
8. The author says, "God made us of clay that has a mind of its own." What are some of the positives and negatives?
9. Name some different ways we serve the King as his vessels.
10. What new insights into being God's vessels did you gain from reading this chapter?

Prayer

Dear God, we thank you for allowing us to be a member of your household and to serve you as you see fit. Remind us that you are the Potter and we are your clay. Help us to serve you in love. Amen.

CHAPTER 5
THE CHRISTIAN'S LARGER FAMILY

Summary

This chapter reminds us that as Christians, we are all family. It tells us how Paul saw his community of believers as family and how he cared for and treated his spiritual children. We also learn why family matters.

Discussion Questions

1. What is known about Paul's family?
2. Explain Paul's family as it existed, as the author put it, "in the world of metaphor."
3. How does Paul assure the Christians in Rome that God accepts them?
4. What is meant by the word *Abba*? How did Paul use the word?
5. Describe the image of God as a father. What was it about the idea of comfort Paul was trying to communicate with this imagery?
6. Paul saw the community of believers as family. What does this mean for us today?
7. In what ways were Paul and other traveling Christians offered hospitality by "family" members?
8. Explain how Paul treated and cared for his spiritual children. Who were some of them by name?

9. How and why do Paul's family metaphors continue today?
10. What does the word family mean to you? Why does family matter?

Prayer

Dear God, thank you for showing us that we are all family and that each one of us matters. Thank you for being a father to us. Help us to treat all people we encounter, even strangers, as family. Amen.

CHAPTER 6
BABIES AND GROWN-UPS TOO

Summary

This chapter begins with the encounter between Jesus and Nicodemus, showing us lessons we can learn from it. We also learn about Paul's conversion and why he uses the metaphor of an infant in his letter to the Corinthians. This chapter also illustrates the goal of new birth and why we all must be born anew.

Discussion Questions

1. What lessons are there for us today in the encounter of Jesus and Nicodemus?
2. Explain why this encounter is so significant and what it says about a second birth.
3. Why, according to the author, is this such a powerful metaphor?
4. What is meant by the phrase "new birth"? Why is this radical change needed?

5. Explain how and why being born again is a beginning and a new way of life.
6. What can we learn about being born again by Paul's conversion on the road to Damascus?
7. Why does Paul use the metaphor of an infant in his letter to the Corinthians?
8. What is the goal of the new birth?
9. Explain Paul's passion for helping Christians to mature in the faith.
10. What is needed in order for us to be born anew?

Prayer

Dear God, thank you for Paul's words about being born again and the reminder that we need to be born anew. Help us to grow from infants into mature Christians through your guidance and encouragement. Amen.

CHAPTER 7
PORTRAITS OF THE CHURCH

Summary

This chapter looks at the Day of Pentecost and how we are the body of the church, which is the body of Christ. Paul calls the church the bride of Christ and shows us how the church is similar to the human body.

Discussion Questions

1. Share what the church means to you and how it has made an impact in your life.

2. Why is the Day of Pentecost referred to as "the birthday of the church"?

3. According to the author, why didn't Paul use a "new nation" metaphor to describe the church?

4. How is the church similar to the human body?

5. What does it mean when we say that the body of the church is the body of Christ?

6. How does Paul describe the church in Ephesians 2:19-21?

7. "We are God's building," according to Paul; explain his reasoning for putting it that way.

8. Why is it most important to remember that the cornerstone of the church is Jesus Christ?

9. Explain why Paul calls the church the bride of Christ.

10. Which of Paul's metaphors most appeals to you?

Prayer

Dear God, thank you for giving us the gift of the church to minister to us and to help us grow spiritually. Remind us that we are the body of Christ, and the church is the bride of Christ. Help us to strengthen and serve your church. Amen.

CHAPTER 8
THE CHRISTIAN AS SOLDIER AND AS ACTOR

Summary

This chapter reminds us of the ongoing war in our world between good and evil. Paul uses images of both a soldier and an actor in his metaphors to help us as we struggle to win this war. We also learn why the Christian life is demanding and what our roles are in fighting life's battles.

Discussion Questions

1. From your own perspective, describe the evidence that there is a war in our world between good and evil.
2. Explain why Paul viewed the Christian life as an "engagement in a continuing conflict."
3. What would you say are some of the biblical and historical high points in the struggle between good and evil?
4. Who were some of the biblical characters involved in this struggle? What sorts of things do you believe they might have had in common?
5. Why is the human soul "the major battleground" in this war?
6. What metaphorical images of warfare did Paul use in his letters?
7. Who is our enemy in this war?
8. How do we deal with evil in our world; what do you believe are some effective strategies?
9. Explain Paul's metaphor of the actor.
10. Give some reasons why the Christian life is "wonderfully demanding."

Prayer

Dear God, thank you for Paul's message encouraging us to stay on our guard, and help us to fight against evil in all its forms. May we join together with other Christians as we strive to make our world a better place. Amen.

CHAPTER 9
PICTURES OF A BAPTISMAL SERVICE

Summary

This chapter is devoted to the act of baptism and what it means to be "baptized into Christ." We learn the metaphors Paul used to explain baptism to converts and the connection between sin and baptism.

Discussion Questions

1. In your own words, describe the importance of baptism.
2. When you attend a baptismal service, what pictures or images do you remember?
3. What impresses you about Paul's conversion and baptism?
4. Explain why "conversion and baptism seem to go hand in hand in the Book of Acts."
5. Why was baptism not emphasized in Paul's ministry?
6. What are some of Paul's metaphors about baptism?
7. What challenges did Paul face in explaining baptism to his converts?
8. What does it mean to be "baptized into Christ"?
9. Give some details about what the author refers to as "Paul's most striking picture of baptism."
10. Explain Paul's understanding of sin and how it is connected to baptism.

Prayer

Dear God, thank you for giving us Paul's insights and teachings regarding baptism. Remind us that we are baptized into

Christ. Help us to remember that we belong to you and that we are here to love and assist others in their journey. Amen.

CHAPTER 10
LESSONS IN LIVING WITH DEFEAT

Summary

This chapter examines the struggles Paul faced throughout his life and ministry and how he dealt with them. We learn what it means to have "a thorn in the flesh" and "a thorn in the spirit" and how to live with disappointments and defeat.

Discussion Questions

1. Describe some of the disappointments and struggles that have shaped your life.
2. Why is it dangerous to dream and hope? What do we stand to lose?
3. Name some of Paul's objectives. What did he want to accomplish?
4. What metaphor did Paul use to name his day-by-day defeat?
5. What does the author say were some of the possible thorns with which Paul may have struggled?
6. Why do you think that Paul never identified what he referred to as his personal "thorn"? What do you think it may have been, and why?
7. How did Paul deal with his thorn? What lessons can we learn from him?
8. Why did Paul consider himself to be a better person with the thorn than without it?

9. What is meant by "a thorn in the spirit"?
10. What do Paul and his teachings tell us about how we should handle defeat in our own lives?

Prayer

Dear God, thank you for the reminder that we will encounter thorns during this life. Help us to remember the struggles of Paul and how he responded to them. May we continue to dream, hope, and help others as we work toward accomplishing your will. Amen.

CHAPTER 11
THE CHRISTIAN LIFE BEYOND WORDS

Summary

This chapter examines some of the memorable spiritual experiences and miracles that Paul experienced during his life and ministry. Paul uses the phrase "the third heaven" to hint at what happened to him. This chapter also shows the many ways Christ comes to us and what it means to be "in Christ."

Discussion Questions

1. Recall a time or an experience in your life that was hard to express in words.
2. Why did some in the early church question Paul's authority?
3. What did Paul say about his "third heaven" religious experience?
4. As this chapter outlines, what were some of the visions Paul had during his ministry?

5. What can we learn about Paul and about God from Paul's visions and experiences?
6. Explain what Paul meant in using "the third heaven" as a descriptive metaphor—why that particular phrase?
7. Paul's goal was to be "in Christ." What did he mean by this?
8. Recall a special or memorable religious experience you've experienced or witnessed.
9. What are some of the ways in which Christ comes to us?
10. What new insight into the Christian life did you gain from this chapter?

Prayer

Dear God, thank you for the special and memorable spiritual experiences of life you provide. Thank you for teaching us more about Paul and his visions. May we also accept Paul's goal to be "in Christ" and to do your will. Amen.

CHAPTER 12
THIS MORTAL AND IMMORTAL FLESH

Summary

This chapter uses the metaphors of Paul to provide insights into our spiritual and physical bodies. We live in "tents," according to Paul, and our bodies are temples of our God. We learn why each temple is sacred and why the human body is a force to be reckoned with.

Discussion Questions

1. Why do you think the Bible says nothing about the physical appearance of Jesus?

2. What is known about Paul's appearance?
3. How and why does the human body present us humans with "unique perils"?
4. What did Paul say about his own human body?
5. Explain why the human body is, as the author suggests Paul would have described it, "a force to be reckoned with."
6. What metaphor did Paul use to describe the human body in its relationship to God, and why was is it so effective?
7. According to the author, why is this Paul's "most daring of metaphors"?
8. How did the Jewish people feel about the sacredness of the temple?
9. Explain why our human bodies are really just "tents," according to Paul.
10. How have you been helped spiritually by reading this book?

Prayer

Dear God, thank you for giving us valuable information about our spiritual and physical bodies. Help us to remember that we all do live in "tents" as we live our lives day to day. Thank you for all we have gained from this book, and help us to continue our spiritual growth. Amen.

9 781630 882532